Day Wa
Cairngorms

20 circular routes
in the Scottish Highlands

Vertebrate Publishing, Sheffield
www.v-publishing.co.uk

Day Walks in the Cairngorms

20 circular routes
in the Scottish Highlands

Helen & Paul Webster

Day Walks in the **Cairngorms**

20 circular routes in the
Scottish Highlands

 First published in 2020 by **Vertebrate Publishing.**

Vertebrate Publishing, Omega Court, 352 Cemetery Road,
Sheffield S11 8FT, United Kingdom.
www.v-publishing.co.uk

A CIP catalogue record for this book is available from the British Library.

ISBN 978-1-912560-63-9

Front cover: Loch an Eilein (route 6).
Back cover: Glen Quoich (route 17).

Photography by **Paul and Helen Webster** unless otherwise credited.

 All maps reproduced by permission of Ordnance Survey on behalf
of The Controller of Her Majesty's Stationery Office.
© Crown Copyright. 100025218

Design by Nathan Ryder, production by Cameron Bonser.

www.**v-publishing**.co.uk

Printed and bound in Europe by Pulsio.

Vertebrate Publishing is committed to printing on paper from sustainable sources.

MIX
Paper from
responsible sources
FSC® C128169
www.fsc.org

Contents

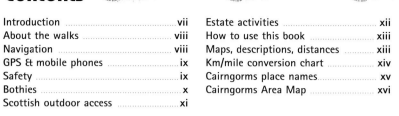

* Shortcut available

GLEN DERRY

Introduction

The Cairngorms is the largest national park in Great Britain, offering a huge variety of landscapes and habitats with endless opportunities for exploring on foot. They include five of the six highest Munros, rising above a vast granite plateau, scoured by winds and encircled by a spectacular array of craggy, glacier-scooped corries. Up here only a handful of specialised animals and birds can survive – including snow bunting, mountain hare and ptarmigan. For hillwalkers the plateau offers a true sense of remote wildness, with challenging navigation and often ferocious weather conditions.

Around this mountain core the landscapes are more accessible yet no less stunning. The Cairngorms include the extensive remains of the vast and ancient Caledonian pinewoods that once swathed much of the Highlands. This is the largest area of native forest surviving in the UK, home to the crested tit, the red squirrel, the crossbill and the endangered capercaillie. After years of decline due to overgrazing, the forests are expanding once more.

The waterscapes too are remarkable. The sparkling, fast-flowing rivers of the Spey and the Dee are legendary for their salmon fishing, and there is an array of beautiful forest lochs and lochans. Here too are the Insh marshes, one of the UK's most important wetlands. Keep an eye out for golden eagles, osprey, hen harriers and buzzards as well as waders such as curlew, lapwings and oyster-catchers who thrive on the rich insect life of the area.

The Cairngorms is very much a living landscape; there is a long and rich heritage and many people are drawn to live and work here by the natural environment. The elemental and restorative power of this landscape is celebrated in Nan Shepherd's evocative book *The Living Mountain* and her face now graces the back of a Scottish £5 note. Today people visit the National Park to walk, climb, mountain bike and ski or to wildlife watch. Ecotourism is often claimed to have started with the return of the ospreys to Loch Garten, and today tourism – including walking and nature watching – is the main driver of the local economy, providing almost half of employment, supported by farming, forestry and the service sector. Whilst large-scale sporting estates still dominate much of the uplands and are managed for grouse and red deer shooting, an increasing amount of the Cairngorms are now managed for conservation. A huge long-term rewilding project, Cairngorms Connect, spans much of the northern flank of the mountains and aims to increase biodiversity and natural forest cover, at the same time as boosting responsible tourism and providing sustainable jobs for the future.

The possibilities in the Cairngorms for an enthusiastic walker are inexhaustible. This book presents an introduction, with 20 stunning circular walks including everything from low-level explorations of the forests and lochs to moorland walks and ascents on to the high plateau to visit the great summits. Enjoy!

Helen & Paul Webster

About the walks

The walks in this book range between 6.3 and 18.4 miles (10.2 and 29.6 kilometres) and will take around four to ten hours at average walking speed without allowing for stops.

The lower-level walks generally follow good paths, although some map reading will be necessary as they are not signed or waymarked throughout. On the upland walks, be prepared for some pathless terrain requiring good navigation skills, particularly in poor weather. For these walks, some previous hillwalking experience is assumed.

Navigation

The Cairngorms are a large area and are covered in full by a number of Ordnance Survey (OS) Explorer 1:25,000 or OS Landranger 1:50,000 maps, while Harvey produce a map covering the heart of the region in their British Mountain Maps range.

The map and description included in this book should be adequate to follow the lower-level routes safely and accurately; however, it is always worth carrying a back-up copy of the relevant OS or Harvey map.

For the higher mountain walks it is essential to carry the relevant map so that you can navigate to safety if you need to leave the intended route. You should also carry a compass and be able to navigate using it on those routes.

The routes in this book are covered by the following maps in the OS 1:25,000 Explorer series:
OL50 Ben Alder, Loch Ericht & Loch Laggan
OL52 Glen Shee & Braemar
OL53 Lochnagar, Glen Muick & Glen Clova
OL56 Badenoch & Upper Strathspey
OL57 Cairn Gorm & Aviemore
OL58 Braemar, Tomintoul & Glen Avon
OL59 Aboyne, Alford & Strathdon
OL61 Grantown-on-Spey & Hills of Cromdale

GPS & mobile phones

A GPS and/or mobile phone with OS-quality mapping installed on the device can be very useful, both for pinpointing your exact position and for checking against a downloaded route. However, do not rely on having mobile phone signal and be aware that batteries can fail on long days; carry back up batteries, leave phones in airplane mode to prolong battery life, and tell someone where you are going and when you plan to get back.

Safety

Well-fitting walking boots will provide the protection and grip your feet need on the mountain routes. Trail shoes may be adequate in dry conditions and on the lower-level routes, although always prepare for some areas of wet ground. Similarly, always carry waterproofs, spare clothing including hat and gloves on mountain walks (even in the summer), food and drink and consider taking a torch and first aid kit.

Sunscreen and a sun hat should be taken in the summer. Midges are usually less of a problem in the Cairngorms than they are on the west coast, but you might want to consider carrying a repellent or midge-net. Ticks, which can spread Lyme disease, are found in the Cairngorms area; carry a tick remover and check yourself at the end of the day. If you are bitten and then develop a 'bullseye' reaction at the bite spot, experience cold-like symptoms or feel unwell seek medical advice.

Mountain weather can change rapidly. Always check the mountain weather forecast and be prepared for cold, windy and wet weather and know how to navigate in low cloud and fog. Sometimes the best decision can be to turn back – keep an eye on the weather and change plans if need be.

Winter conditions
The walks are described for summer conditions. Winter mountain walking comes with its own challenges. The days are short; a headtorch and spare batteries should be part of your kit. When snow and icy conditions are forecast you must carry, and know how to use, crampons and an ice axe. Check the Scottish Avalanche Information Service for current avalanche risks, plan your route accordingly and be prepared to change it. Navigation can be much harder when there are no paths visible on the ground. Attending a winter skills course is highly recommended, or at least go with more experienced people until you have the skills. Ensure that you have enough warm clothes and tell someone where you plan to go.

Rescue
In case of an emergency dial **999** and ask for **Police** and then **Mountain Rescue**. Where possible give a six-figure grid reference of your location or that of your casualty. If you don't have mobile reception try to attract the attention of others nearby. The standard distress signal is six short blasts on a whistle every minute.

Emergency rescue by SMS text
In the UK you can also contact the emergency services by SMS text – useful if you have low battery or intermittent signal. You need to register your phone first by texting '**register**' to **999** and then following the instructions in the reply. **Do it now** – it could save yours or someone else's life. **www.emergencysms.org.uk**

Bothies
Bothies are unlocked shelters in remote locations throughout Scotland where hillwalkers, climbers and mountain bikers are able to spend the night. They range from rough stone shelters to disused cottages with several rooms. The Mountain Bothies Association is a registered charity taking care of around 100 bothies. Visit **www.mountainbothies.org.uk** for more information.

Scottish outdoor access

Scotland's 'right to roam' law gives walkers rights of access over most land away from residential buildings. These rights come with responsibilities which are set out in the Scottish Outdoor Access Code (**www.outdooraccess-scotland.scot**) and summarised here.

Take personal responsibility for your own actions. You can do this by:

» caring for your own safety by recognising that the outdoors is a working environment and by taking account of natural hazards;

» taking special care if you are responsible for children as a parent, teacher or guide to ensure that they enjoy the outdoors responsibly and safely.

Respect people's privacy and peace of mind. You can do this by:

» using a path or track, if there is one, when you are close to a house or garden;

» if there is no path or track, by keeping a sensible distance from houses and avoiding ground that overlooks them from close by;

» taking care not to act in ways which might annoy or alarm people living in a house; and

» at night, taking extra care by keeping away from buildings where people might not be expecting to see anyone and by following paths and tracks.

Help land managers and others to work safely and effectively. You can do this by:

» not hindering a land management operation, by keeping a safe distance and following any reasonable advice from the land manager;

» following any precautions taken or reasonable recommendations made by the land manager, such as to avoid an area or route when hazardous operations, such as tree felling and crop spraying, are under way;

» checking to see what alternatives there are, such as neighbouring land, before entering a field of animals;

» never feeding farm animals;

» avoiding causing damage to crops by using paths or tracks, by going round the margins of the field, by going on any unsown ground or by considering alternative routes on neighbouring ground; and by

» leaving all gates as you find them.

Care for your environment. You can do this by:
» not intentionally or recklessly disturbing or destroying plants, birds and other animals, or geological features;
» following any voluntary agreements between land managers and recreation bodies;
» not damaging or disturbing cultural heritage sites;
» not causing any pollution and by taking all your litter away with you.

Keep your dog under proper control. You can do this by:
» never letting it worry or attack livestock;
» never taking it into a field where there are calves or lambs;
» keeping it on a short lead or under close control in fields where there are farm animals;
» if cattle react aggressively and move towards you, by keeping calm, letting the dog go and taking the shortest, safest route out of the field;
» keeping it on a short lead or under close control during the bird breeding season (usually April to July) in areas such as moorland, forests, grassland, loch shores and the seashore;
» picking up and removing any faeces if your dog defecates in a public open place.

Estate activities

Despite many people's objections on conservation and ethical grounds, shooting remains an important source of income for Highland estates and provides employment for rural communities. As part of exercising our right to access the countryside responsibly, we must take the interests of these landowners into account.

Red deer stalking season runs from 1 July to 20 October for stags, and from 21 October to 15 February for hinds. The majority of stalking that may affect hillwalkers is undertaken between August and October. Grouse shooting begins on 12 August, running until 10 December, with most activity earlier in the season.

Within this period, individual estates will have their own stalking times and locations, so please find out where stalking is taking place before planning your route. The Heading for the Scottish Hills scheme replaces the previous Hillphones scheme and provides up-to-date information on where and when stalking is taking place. Not all upland areas are included

in the scheme: some sporting estates do not participate and in others stalking is absent.
For more information please visit: **www.outdooraccess-scotland.scot**

How to use this book

This book should provide you with all the information you need for an enjoyable, trouble-free and successful walk. The following tips should help:

1. We strongly recommend that you invest in the relevant OS or Harvey map for the walk in case you need to cut short the walk or take an alternative route. A map should be considered essential if you are tackling any of the mountain routes.

2. Choose your route carefully taking into account the time available, abilities and experience of all those in your group and weather forecast – read the safety section of this guide.

3. We recommend that you study the route description carefully before setting off. Cross-reference this with your map so that you've got a good sense of general orientation in case you need an escape route. Make sure that you are familiar with the symbols used on the maps.

4. Get out there and get walking!

Maps, descriptions, distances

While every effort has been made to maintain accuracy within the maps and descriptions in this guide, we have had to process a vast amount of information and we are unable to guarantee that every single detail is correct. Please exercise caution if a direction appears at odds with the route on the map. If in doubt, a comparison between the route, the description and a quick cross-reference with your map (along with a bit of common sense) should help ensure that you're on the right track.

Note that distances have been measured off the map, and map distances rarely coincide 100 per cent with distances on the ground. Please treat stated distances as a guideline only. Ordnance Survey maps are the most commonly used, are easy to read and many people are happy using them. If you're not familiar with OS maps and are unsure of what the symbols mean, you can download a free OS 1:25,000 map legend from **www.ordnancesurvey.co.uk**

Here are a few of the symbols and abbreviations we use on the maps and in our directions:

 ROUTE STARTING POINT   **ROUTE MARKER**   **SHORTCUT**

 **OPTIONAL ROUTE**   **ADDITIONAL GRID LINE NUMBERS TO AID NAVIGATION**

FP = Footpath   **GR** = Grid reference
LHS/LH = Left-hand side/Left-hand   **RHS/RH** = Right-hand side/Right-hand
(!) = Caution

Km/mile conversion chart

Metric to Imperial

1 kilometre [km]	1,000 m	0.6214 mile
1 metre [m]	100 cm	1.0936 yd
1 centimetre [cm]	10 mm	0.3937 in
1 millimetre [mm]		0.03937 in

Imperial to Metric

1 mile	1,760 yd	1.6093 km
1 yard [yd]	3 ft	0.9144 m
1 foot [ft]	12 in	0.3048 m
1 inch [in]		2.54 cm

Cairngorms place names

Many of the place names in the Cairngorms and the words used to describe the landscape derive from the Gaelic language with a little Scots and Norse sometimes thrown in for good measure. Here is a short glossary of the some of the words you may encounter.

àirigh	shieling or summer shelter	eas	waterfall
allt	stream	fada	long
baile	town or settlement	fasgadh	shelter
bàn/bhàn	white	fraoch	heather
beag	small	glas	grey or green
bealach	mountain pass, col or shoulder	làirig	pass or facing slope of hill
bein/beinn	hill, mountain or peak	loch	lake
brae	slope	lochan	small lake
burn	stream	meall	rounded hill
càrn/chàrn	stony hill	meikle/mòr/mhòr	big
clais	gorge or ravine	mullach	summit
cnoc	small hill or knoll	òrd	cone-shaped hill
coire	corrie	ruadh	red
creag	crag, rock or cliff	sgurr/sgorr	peak
dearg	red	srath/strath	valley
druim	ridge	stùc	pinnacle, peak
dubh	black or dark	tigh/taigh	house
dun	fort		

SECTION 1

Badenoch & the Western Cairngorms

The A9 leads down from the bare Drumochter Pass into Badenoch – the uppermost part of the River Spey catchment. The hills either side of the pass, and the Monadhliath to the north, are mostly rounded but offer superb views towards the main Cairngorm peaks and vast skies.

The strath itself is full of interest; the huge ruins of Ruthven Barracks guarding the entrance to the bird haven of the Insh Marshes and the nearby lively villages of Kingussie and Newtonmore. To the east is Glen Feshie, to many the finest of all Cairngorm glens – a nature lover's dream, and the heart of a vast rewilding project.

VIEW OVER BADENOCH FROM CREAGAN AN FHITHICH

LOOKING OVER NEWTONMORE FROM CREAG BHEAG

01 **Creag Bheag & the Wildcat Trail** 18.8km/11.7miles

This satisfying loop explores the wee rocky hill of Creag Bheag above Kingussie taking in a loch, open moorland and a beautiful stretch of riverside.

Kingussie » Creag Bheag » Loch Gynack » Allt Laraidh » Calder Path » River Spey » Highland Folk Museum » Kingussie

Start
Ardvonie car park, Kingussie.
GR: NH 755007.

The Walk

This exploration of the rivers and moorland sandwiched between the high mountains of the Cairngorms and Monadhliath combines a surprising variety of landscapes around the two villages of Newtonmore and Kingussie. There is also a chance to visit the superb Highland Folk Museum.

The route starts from Kingussie, which has a mix of shops, cafes and galleries. It crosses a park and climbs past some impressive Victorian villas before taking a path up through pinewoods and out on to the moors. The heather-clad ridge of Creag Bheag has great character, and the summit itself is marked with a large cairn and stone seat providing fine views over much of Badenoch and towards the Cairngorms. The hill is a much-loved part of the Highland community, its crags popular with climbers, and its summit the objective of a hill race held every September.

A steep and rough descent path leads down to the trees above Loch Gynack. The route then turns west, following a track through open moorland with expansive views to the Monadhliath mountains. This is a good place to spot birds of prey including buzzards, golden eagles and the rare hen harrier.

The walk then joins the Wildcat Trail, a circular route enclosing the neighbouring settlement of Newtonmore. Keeping high above the village, a series of paths lead through mixed woodland to reach a stunning stretch of path overlooking the River Calder. At this point it is possible to detour into Newtonmore where there are shops, cafes and pubs. The walk itself follows the Calder downstream to reach the mighty River Spey, eventually skirting the golf course to head through the edge of the Highland Folk Museum, based in a series of relocated historic buildings. Entrance is free and it is well worth allowing time to explore. Finally, a shared cycleway leads back to Kingussie and the start of the walk.

CREAG BHEAG & THE WILDCAT TRAIL

DISTANCE: 18.8KM/11.7 MILES » **TOTAL ASCENT:** 364M/1,194FT » **START GR:** NH 755007 » **TIME:** ALLOW 6.5 HOURS » **SATNAV:** PH21 1EZ » **MAP:** OS EXPLORER 56, BADENOCH & UPPER STRATHSPEY, 1:25,000 » **REFRESHMENTS:** SUGAR BOWL CAFE, KINGUSSIE, OR THE GLEN HOTEL, NEWTONMORE » **NAVIGATION:** STRAIGHTFORWARD ON MOSTLY CLEAR PATHS.

**01 CREAG BHEAG &
THE WILDCAT TRAIL**

Directions – Creag Bheag & the Wildcat Trail

➎ From the Ardvonie car park behind the Duke of Gordon Hotel, pass to the right of the toilets and cross the grass following the sign for *Creag Bheag Summit*. **Turn right** at the road and soon **bear left** on to a track. Go **straight ahead** through two gates and climb through pinewoods, ignoring paths on the left keeping on the waymarked path. **Go through a gate** to leave the woods and soon **turn right** to follow the moorland path eventually reaching the summit of Creag Bheag. After the final cairn and seat **keep ahead** as the path starts to descend, with a couple of rocky and steep sections.

2 Lower down arrive at a signposted junction; **turn left** to follow a path above Loch Gynack signed *Newtonmore*. When the wide path reaches a track, **turn left** along it with the distant mountains of the Monadhliath visible ahead. At the next track junction **keep left** again and continue across the moor until a farm gate comes into view. Ignore a track off left, **keeping ahead** to pass through the gate. Follow the track towards a forestry plantation. Here, at a turning circle with a gate on the edge of the trees, **continue ahead on to a path** alongside the trees, **crossing a footbridge**. At the far corner of the plantation go through a gate and immediately **turn left** on to a path through the heather. The path eventually runs alongside a stream. **Keep straight ahead** when it joins a track and later **cross a footbridge** near a ford. Continue along the track until after a sheepfold, then **turn right** to cross another footbridge and **aim uphill** towards a gate at the corner of a wood.

3 Go through the gate into the wood and **keep straight on** following the path along the edge of the trees. Cross a number of gates and stiles before a row of marker stones indicate where to **bear half-left** to a gate. Go through it and **keep straight on*** at a marker post, soon reaching another gate and joining an often-muddy track ahead through the trees. **Keep left** at a fork and go through a farm gate. Stay on the track as it curves left and then **go straight ahead** through another farm gate, soon passing a white cottage. **Keep straight ahead** at the cottage to reach a road. **Turn right** following the *Wildcat Trail* signs and head uphill on the road.

☾ ***SC: Turn left** at the marker post to shortcut directly to Newtonmore where you can **turn left** along Main Street to pass the Highland Folk Museum and rejoin the route back to Kingussie.

4 A short way after a cattle grid **turn right** at a wildcat marker to reach woodland. **Climb the stile** and follow the path through birches and pine forestry. At a gate and track **turn left** along a wide break in the trees and go through a kissing gate to return to the road. **Turn right** along it. As views up Glen Banchor open up ahead **fork left** on to the *Calder Path*. The grassy path undulates and passes through a gate before a dramatic section high above the River Calder. Don't pass through the next gate but **turn right** downhill to soon run alongside the cemetery before climbing up to another gate and a small wood to reach a stile and bench at the A86.

5 **Go straight across** the road on to the track opposite. Go through the gate on the right to reach the riverside path. Follow the Calder until it meets the River Spey and **pass under the road bridge** after a stile. The path keeps to the riverbank passing under the railway; go through a number of gates and stiles **keeping on the path near the river**. Eventually the route passes the golf course and the path **bears left** away from the river. **Cross a footbridge** and then another and **bear left to climb uphill** to go over the railway.

> **OR** If the Calder is in flood and the riverbank path is impassable, where the Calder meets the Spey **take the high stile on the left** and then **bear right** to cross fields before **another stile on the right** brings you back to the riverbank beyond the flood-prone section.

6 At a junction **continue straight ahead** to reach Main Street. **Turn right,** soon passing the main entrance to the Highland Folk Museum. This is well worth a visit and it can easily take two hours to explore all the reconstructed buildings which include a thatched black-house village. Otherwise, continue for a short distance and then **bear right** on to the shared cycle path. Follow this all the way into Kingussie. **Turn left** to cross the road after the Duke of Gordon Hotel and **turn left** again to return to the car park at the start.

CÀRN DEARG MÒR FROM GLEN FESHIE

DISTANCE: 23.2KM/14.4MILES » **TOTAL ASCENT:** 650M/2,133FT » **START GR:** NN 850985 » **TIME:** ALLOW 8 HOURS
SATNAV: PH21 1NH » **MAP:** OS EXPLORER 57, CAIRN GORM & AVIEMORE, 1:25,000 » **REFRESHMENTS:** NONE ON
ROUTE » **NAVIGATION:** REQUIRES NAVIGATION SKILLS, INCLUDES PATHLESS SECTION THROUGH HEATHER.

GLEN FESHIE

02 Càrn Dearg Mòr from Glen Feshie 23.2km/14.4miles

Explore Càrn Dearg Mòr, a Corbett forming much of the west flank of beautiful Glen Feshie.

Achlean Car Park » Glen Feshie Bridge » Carnachuin » Ruigh-fionntaig » Slochd Mòr » Càrn Dearg Mòr » Càrn Dearg Beag » Glen Feshie Bridge » Achlean

Start

Car park on east side of Glen Feshie, one kilometre north of Achlean. GR: NN 850985.

The Walk

The walkers' car park just north of Achlean is a popular starting point for many different routes, both up on to the Moine Mhor plateau and through Glen Feshie. This route combines characteristics of both, starting by heading past the farm at Achlean and then following a path up the glen, soon crossing to the far side.

Glen Feshie is being managed for woodland restoration and wildlife as the jewel in the crown amongst the estates owned by Anders Povlsen, one of Scotland's largest landowners. The area is part of an ambitious 600-square-kilometre rewilding project known as Cairngorms Connect, which combines Mr Povlsen's land with neighbouring estates owned by the RSPB, NatureScot and Forestry Land Scotland. As the route heads up the glen the results of this conservation-friendly management become apparent. There are large and spectacularly beautiful areas of naturally regenerating native pinewoods, with rich birdlife and wildlife, achieved mostly through reducing the red deer population to more natural levels.

Once past the cottages at Carnachuin and Glen Feshie Lodge the route climbs through the deep defile of the Slochd Mòr, passing a lovely lochan. From the col beyond a moorland track climbs up on to the broad and open ridge, from where a short further climb leads to the summit of Càrn Dearg Mòr. At 857 metres this hill is classed as a Corbett – a Scottish mountain between 2,500 and 3,000 feet with at least 500 feet of descent all the way round. Increasingly popular with those who have already climbed the 282 Scottish Munros, the 222 Corbetts present a tough challenge to hill baggers.

From the summit the route descends the broad north ridge to the top of Càrn Dearg Beag (beag actually means small in Gaelic, while mòr means big). A further heathery descent leads to a track which doubles back before heading through superb pinewoods down into Glen Feshie. Once back in the glen the outward route is retraced to return to the start.

02 CÀRN DEARG MÒR
FROM GLEN FESHIE

Directions – Càrn Dearg Mòr from Glen Feshie

➎ From the car park **turn left** to continue up the road towards the farm at Achlean, ignoring a path heading off left through the heather. Just before the farmhouse **bear left** on to a surfaced path and continue past the farm, ignoring smaller paths off on either side. **Pass through a gate and cross the burn** beyond – there is no bridge and the crossing can be a problem in spate. The path now follows the edge of a heather bank high above the wide and braided flood plain which shows the channels the Feshie takes when in spate.

2 **Fork right** at a junction to head towards and **cross the footbridge** over the Feshie visible ahead. Head uphill on a short section of track and **turn left** on to the surfaced private road. After 2km pass an estate cottage and **continue ahead** to pass the farm and houses at Carnachuin. **Continue straight ahead** where a track leads off to the left – a bridge used to cross the Feshie here but was washed away in a storm. **Fork left** on to a track when the drive to Glen Feshie Lodge branches to the right.

3 In 2km at another junction **branch right** to take the track heading up into the Slochd Mòr. *Slochd* is Gaelic meaning a slot or pass and this deep trench makes an unusual feature as the route climbs out of Glen Feshie. The track climbs past Lochan an t-Sluic. **Fork right** at the next junction to follow a track as it zigzags uphill keeping well to the right of the forestry plantations. **Bend left** on the track above the plantation and after it becomes much less steep **turn right** on to a rough path which climbs steadily up to the heather-clad ridge. **Fork right** to follow the broad ridge north-east to reach the summit of Càrn Dearg Mòr, a fantastic viewpoint overlooking Badenoch and Strathspey to the north.

4 **Continue ahead,** on a faint track at first, to descend the ridge. The going becomes pathless; climb slightly and **keep west** of the trig point marking the top of Càrn Dearg Beag. Continue ahead down the ridge and soon the route again becomes pathless. Stay on the ridge as it **curves north–north–east** and keep heading downhill over rougher ground until a track is reached just before a forestry plantation.

5 **Turn right** to follow the track through stunning ancient pinewoods to arrive in Glen Feshie just beyond Carnachuin, rejoining the outward route. **Turn left** to retrace your steps along the road and after 2.5km **bear right** to cross the footbridge over the Feshie. On the far side **turn left** to return to Achlean and **keep straight on** here to reach the start.

UATH LOCHANS

03 **Feshiebridge & the Uath Lochans** 12.2km/7.6miles

This beautiful and varied walk includes a stunning stretch of the River Feshie, a classic view overlooking the Uath Lochans, Loch Insh, and the fascinating sculptures of Frank Bruce.

Feshiebridge » Ballintean » Uath Lochans » Loch Insh » Frank Bruce Sculpture Park » Feshiebridge

Start

Frank Bruce Sculpture Park car park (parking charge), B970, north-west of Feshiebridge. NH 849046.

The Walk

The circuit starts near the picturesque Feshiebridge, where the River Feshie squeezes through a rocky gorge. From this beauty spot, tracks and paths follow a stunning stretch of riverside upstream. Scattered trees and open clearings are the foreground to the steep slopes of the Cairngorms behind; a wild setting and a haunt of ospreys in the summer.

After leaving the Feshie at Ballintean the route heads through Inshriach Forest to reach the beautiful hidden Uath Lochans, home to rare dragonflies. From here the path climbs steeply to reveal a breathtaking viewpoint looking out over the four watery lochans – a classic panorama capturing all the magic of the Cairngorms.

The route continues along more forest paths before heading towards the much larger Loch Insh. Popular with water sports enthusiasts and fishermen, this is also home to a pair of nesting ospreys. The walk passes the Loch Insh Outdoor Centre which has a restaurant overlooking the water. A short section of farmland leads back to the River Feshie and yet another highlight. Here, amidst the trees, are the fascinating wooden creations of the late sculptor Frank Bruce. Intriguing and sometimes disturbing, these wood and stone works of art depict serious themes of the modern world and are designed to age naturally in their outdoor setting.

FESHIEBRIDGE & THE UATH LOCHANS

DISTANCE: 12.2KM/7.6MILES » **TOTAL ASCENT:** 220M/722FT » **START GR:** NH 849046 » **TIME:** ALLOW 4 HOURS » **SATNAV:** PH21 1NG » **MAP:** OS EXPLORER 57, CAIRN GORM & AVIEMORE, 1:25,000 » **REFRESHMENTS:** THE BOATHOUSE RESTAURANT, LOCH INSH OUTDOOR CENTRE ON ROUTE, OR SHORT DETOUR TO OLD POST OFFICE CAFE, KINCRAIG » **NAVIGATION:** STRAIGHTFORWARD PATHS AND TRACKS.

Directions – Feshiebridge & the Uath Lochans

❺ From the Feshiebridge car park take the **yellow waymarked path** slightly uphill passing a telegraph pole. At Feshiebridge head up to the road and **cross it,** and take the track signed *Rights of Way to Deeside.* **Keep left** to pass a cottage and continue on a narrow track. **Fork left** to go through a gate and soon **fork left** again (arrow marker) to descend on a grassy track. Pass a shed and **go straight ahead** through a gate before the track **bears left** and crosses a small ford.

2 **Keep ahead** as the path runs close to the River Feshie, an area where osprey can often be seen in the late spring and summer months. Go through a wooden gate and **bear right** on the waymarked footpath well before the house at Ballintean. **Keep right** to follow the edge of the lawn and head slightly uphill on a path, emerging next to a house on the right at a junction of tracks. **Go straight across** and follow a track passing to the left of a bungalow. **Keep straight ahead** to pass a house and continue ahead on a track through the trees. A track joins from the left; soon after **branch right** as the track forks and reaches the tarred road. **Turn right** for a short distance then **turn left** on to a forestry track passing a vehicle barrier.

3 **Stay on the main track** when it bends right and again when a white waymarked path joins from the right at a boulder. After the next bend there are views of the first lochan; take the next white waymarked path on the **right.** Continue through the trees to a path junction and **turn left uphill,** now on a broader path, following red waymarkers. **Turn right** at the next junction and climb Farleitter Crag to reach a couple of viewpoints over the Uath Lochans below. **Continue** on the path; **bear left** at a seat and boulder and **keep right** at a waymarked junction. Soon **turn right** at a T-junction and **keep straight ahead** through a forestry plantation when the Badenoch Way leaves to the left. **Bear right** at another T-junction now following *Badenoch Way* signs slightly downhill through a broad gap in the trees, passing a bench. When the path bends right into the trees, **turn left** on to a narrower path which descends to a track.

03 FESHIEBRIDGE & THE UATH LOCHANS

Directions – Feshiebridge & the Uath Lochans continued...

4 **Turn left** here and just before a gate near the B970 road, **fork right** on to a footpath. This keeps close to the road before emerging at a gate near a house. **Bear left** to cross the road diagonally, **take the waymarked path** into the woods on the far side of an entrance drive. Follow the *Badenoch Way* signs as the route **bears right**, then **turns left** at a junction to descend close to Loch Insh. **Fork right** to follow the lochside for a short distance; **fork right up steps** on to a tree-covered ridge before steps continue downwards. **Continue ahead** after a footbridge up steps and **go straight ahead** at a crossroads of paths to soon emerge at the road; **turn left**.

5 **Turn left** a short distance along the road to follow a waymarked path between the entrances to two houses on the edge of Loch Insh. The fenced path descends past the children's play area to reach the car park of Loch Insh Outdoor Centre; **keep to the right** of the Boathouse building and at the road **turn left** on to a path. Soon **turn right** to cross the road and **bear left** on to a path next to a sports field. At the next junction take the **second track on the right** signed *Feshiebridge* (continue ahead to detour to Kincraig). **Continue ahead;** after the building on the right but before the gate **turn right** on to a grassy track.

OSPREY

6 **Keep straight ahead** to go through two farm gates and before the next gate **branch right** to go through another gate and immediately **bear left** on a footpath. Follow the path through trees to a walkers' gate and **keep ahead** with a field on the right. **Keep straight on** when a path joins from the left and soon the entrance to the Frank Bruce Sculpture Park is reached on the right*. The route continues ahead until a path on the **left** signed for the car park returns to the start.

> *To visit the Frank Bruce Sculpture Park, **turn right** through the gate into the walled garden to follow a number of looped paths past the sculptures. Information boards explain each work of art and there is a map at the entrance, but keep **bearing left** to return to the car park entrance track and then **bear right** before **forking left** on the signed path down to the car park.

REFLECTIONS AT UATH LOCHANS

LOOKING OVER LOCH ERICHT

Geal-Charn & A' Mharconaich   11.5km/7.1miles

These two relatively straightforward Munros give great views to mighty Ben Alder and the ranges of the central Highlands.

Balsporran » Cairn on NE Ridge » Geal-Charn Summit » Bealach at 739m » A' Mharconaich Summit » A' Mharconaich NE Ridge » Balsporran

Start
Car park off A9 just north of Drumochter summit near Balsporran Cottages. GR: NN 627791.

The Walk
The effort needed to climb this pair of Munros is greatly reduced by the high starting point on the A9 road through the Drumochter Pass. This makes them a popular pair for those looking to increase their hill tally early in their bagging career. The hills may appear to be heathery lumps from the A9, but their traverse offers grand views.

Balsporran Cottages, not far below the top of the pass, provides a perfect head start at 423 metres above sea level. A track leads past the lonely cottage at Balsporran, now a bed and breakfast, and after crossing the railway line the route heads towards the clear ridge leading to the summit of the first Munro, Geal-Charn – with a path for much of the way. The summit itself is an excellent viewpoint out of all proportion to the effort involved, with Loch Ericht, Ben

Alder and a seemingly endless sea of mountains stretching out to the west.

Keep an eye out for mountain hares, an animal adapted to its high upland habitat with a pelt of thick fur which turns snow white in the winter. Another species totally at home in the high tops is the ptarmigan, a grouse rarely found far below Munro height and which – like the hare – turns white to match the winter snowfalls. Listen out for its distinctive croaking cry.

From Geal-Charn a straightforward descent leads to the wide shoulder from where a featureless plod uphill is rewarded by the increasingly extensive views from the plateau, and eventually the summit of A' Mharconaich is reached, the higher of the two Munros. The descent is quite steep initially, and careful navigation is needed in poor conditions. After this the route down becomes gentler, with a last area of tiring undulating ground to cross before the return to the start at Balsporran.

GEAL-CHARN & A' MHARCONAICH
DISTANCE: 11.5KM/7.1MILES » **TOTAL ASCENT:** 731M/2,398FT » **START GR:** NN 627791 » **TIME:** ALLOW 6 HOURS **SATNAV:** PH19 1AF » **MAP:** OS EXPLORER 50, BEN ALDER, LOCH ERICHT & LOCH LAGGAN, 1:25,000 » **REFRESHMENTS:** NONE ON ROUTE, NEAREST IS SNACK SHACK, DALWHINNIE » **NAVIGATION:** STRAIGHTFORWARD IN GOOD WEATHER, GOOD MAP-READING SKILLS NEEDED IN POOR CONDITIONS.

ON THE PLATEAU NEAR A' MHARCONAICH

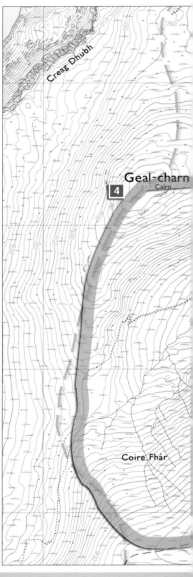

Creag Dhubh

Geal-charn

4 Cairn

Coire Fhàr

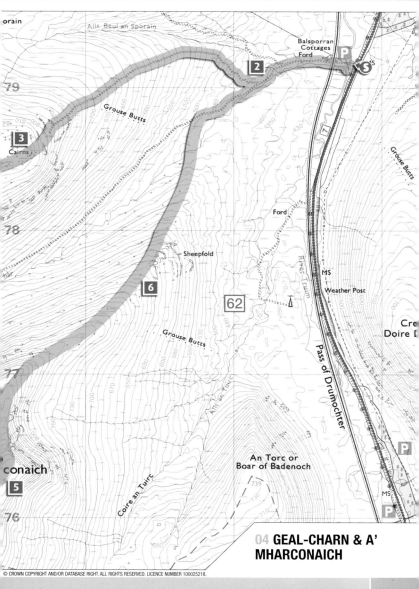

04 **GEAL-CHARN & A'
MHARCONAICH**

Directions – Geal-Charn & A' Mharconaich

⊙➤ From the parking area **turn left** and cross the River Truim before passing the house at Balsporran. Take care on the railway level crossing and on the far side **go straight ahead** on the track. Soon **keep left** where another track forks right. At the stream continue and **cross the bridge**.

2 **Branch right** at the next junction to start climbing towards the north-east ridge of Geal-Charn. Higher up on the broad ridge the track turns into a path through the heather moorland.

3 Where the gradient levels off there was once a set of large cairns, now only one main cairn remains. From here it is a straightforward 1km **hike along the heathery ridge** to the summit of Geal-Charn. It has a great view over Loch Ericht to the large Ben Alder massif and also to its namesake, the other Geal-Chàrn, which is a much tougher undertaking. Looking south the profile of A' Mharconaich is revealed.

4 From the summit **head downhill south-west** at first and then **bear more directly south** to reach the wide shoulder, or bealach, at 739m, which has a track running over it. Cross this and on the far side **continue ahead** to climb uphill until you **bear slight left** at 800m. Although the featureless slope can be daunting at first, it doesn't take long to reach the summit plateau from where the views to Ben Alder are superb. **Continue north-east** and cross the plateau.

5 Soon the summit cairn of A' Mharconaich at 975m, the second Munro of the day, is reached. The descent from the top is steep and care should be taken in poor visibility or winter conditions to find the right route. **Aim north downhill** on a spur with a steep corrie on the right. The spur soon flattens out and then steepens again: stay on it to **bear north-east**.

6 Descend more gently before heading over the rough, pathless and sometimes boggy ground of the lower slopes. **Bear left and cross a stream** (there is a footbridge further downstream if this is not crossable) to pick up a path leading back to Balsporran Cottages and the start.

ABOVE LOCH EINICH

05 **Sgòr Gaoith Circuit**

18km/11.2miles

This airy summit ranks with the most dramatic in all the Cairngorms, perched atop crags that plunge to Loch Einich.

Allt Ruadh parking, Glen Feshie » Allt nam Bò » Allt Coire na Cloiche » Allt a' Chrom-alltain » Sgòr Gaoith » A' Chailleach » Coire Fhearnagan » Achlean » Allt Ruadh parking, Glen Feshie

Start

Car park by Allt Ruadh bridge, east side of Glen Feshie. GR: NH 853012.

The Walk

The Cairngorm mountains hide their finest features from the roads around their base, often appearing as big rounded domes. This classic walk is one of the shorter routes that gives a true taste of the mountain grandeur at the heart of the range. The ascent uses a good path for most of the way, but the approach to the summit of Sgòr Gaoith crosses a featureless and exposed plateau before continuing along a dramatic cliff edge, heavily corniced by snow in winter.

To reach the start take the road up the east side of Glen Feshie, passing Cairngorm Gliding Club. Just before the bridge over the Allt Ruadh take a track on the left to reach a parking area. The walk climbs gently at first through a plantation, the packed trees soon replaced by native birches and finally ancient Scots pine. Some of these majestic, red-barked trees with their twisted branches and wide-girth trunks are likely to be many hundreds of years old and may well have once been brushed by wolves, now long extinct in Scotland. Glen Feshie is now managed for conservation and ecological restoration. The fragments of native forest are regenerating and recovering their former glory, following work in reducing the excessive numbers of deer.

Above the tree line the route follows a path which climbs steadily over moorland, petering out before it reaches the spacious plateau. From here the true drama of the Cairngorms is revealed as the route reaches the steep cliff edge with views down to Loch Einich and follows it for the final climb to the summit of Sgòr Gaoith, a Munro.

The return takes in the rim of these great crags, bypassing Càrn Bàn Mòr before picking up an excellent path which descends back into Glen Feshie to reach the road at Achlean. A pleasant walk along a quiet road leads back to the start.

SGÒR GAOITH CIRCUIT

DISTANCE: 18KM/11.2MILES » **TOTAL ASCENT:** 902M/2,959FT » **START GR:** NH 853012 » **TIME:** ALLOW 7 HOURS
SATNAV: PH21 1NH » **MAP:** OS EXPLORER 57, CAIRN GORM & AVIEMORE, 1:25,000 » **REFRESHMENTS:** NONE ON ROUTE
NAVIGATION: PLATEAU WITH PATHLESS SECTIONS REQUIRES ACCURATE MAP AND COMPASS WORK IN POOR VISIBILITY.

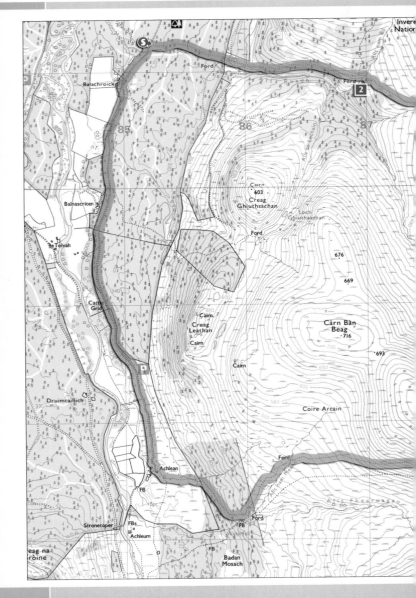

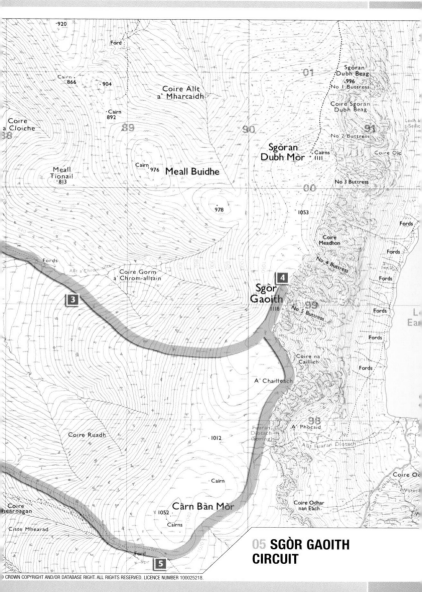

05 SGÒR GAOITH CIRCUIT

Directions – Sgòr Gaoith Circuit

➎ Take the track at the back of the parking area, soon passing a large boulder. At a junction **fork left** on to a good footpath, climbing above the Allt Ruadh which can be glimpsed between the mature pines. As the route climbs views back to the Monadhliath hills can be seen on the far side of Strathspey.

2 Keep **straight ahead** where a path branches left, descending to **cross the Allt nan Bò**. The path now climbs through open heather moorland although some regenerating small pines can also be seen. Continue ahead on the clear path to **cross the Allt Coire na Cloiche**. Follow the path as it traverses the hillside, climbing steadily before eventually reaching the Allt a' Chrom-alltain. Climb alongside the stream for a short distance before **crossing** it.

3 The path continues to climb in a southeasterly direction before it peters out at a height of 810m. Now **bear left** to climb more directly east-south-east to reach the ridge just short of the summit of Sgòr Gaoith. From here there are great views down to Loch Einich, across to Braeriach opposite, and the broken crags of Sgòr Gaoith itself. Keep well back from the precipitous edge, especially in snowy conditions when large overhanging cornices can form here; **bear left** to climb up to the summit at 1118m.

4 From the summit **retrace your steps** for a short distance and then follow the path along the edge of the cliffs to the prow of A' Chailleach. Continue along the rim of the plateau before contouring **south-west** on a pathless section to cross the flank of Càrn Bàn Mòr. Continue to **meet a wide path** that crosses the plateau.

5 **Turn right** to head west on this path, descending north-west back down into Glen Feshie. Much further down the path crosses the Allt nam Meann. **Continue on the path downhill** – there are good views to the upper reaches of Glen Feshie on the left and soon the path leads through trees. At the far edge of the trees **go through a gate** and follow the path to the road. **Turn right,** soon passing the Achlean car park. Continue ahead on the road for approximately 3km to return to the start.

SECTION 2

Aviemore & the Northern Cairngorms

The central Cairngorms present an impressive face to Strathspey and Aviemore, a great wall of mountains sculpted by rugged corries. They provide the backdrop to the great green carpet of Rothiemurchus Forest, dotted by picturesque lochs amongst the Scots pines.

This is the best known part of the Cairngorms National Park, and one of the finest in Scotland for walks at all levels; the wildlife watching opportunities are superb.

THE NORTHERN CORRIES IN WINTER

LOCH AN EILEIN

Be at one with nature in this wildlife-filled circuit of magnificent native forest and lochs.

Coylumbridge » Cairngorm Club Footbridge » Lochan Deò » Loch an Eilein » Ord Bàn »
Loch an Eilein gate » Blackpark » Coylumbridge

Start

Lay-by on B970 just west of Coylumbridge. GR: NH 914106.

The Walk

Acclaimed by Sir David Attenborough as 'one of the glories of wild Scotland', the vast pinewoods of Rothiemurchus are as close to their natural state as you'll find anywhere. Wizened granny pines rub shoulders with teenage saplings, while a thick understorey of juniper and heather supports a rich array of wildlife. Keep an eye out for red squirrels, crested tits, crossbills and the elusive capercaillie as you explore the forest and lochs.

The route follows good paths and is almost flat except for the optional rougher ascent to Ord Bàn, from where you can survey the whole forest and take in the stunning mountain views. This walk is a good option when cloud shrouds the peaks or when a lower level, easier walk is needed. Due to ground nesting birds, dogs need to be kept on the paths, preferably on a lead, between April and August.

Starting from Coylumbridge just outside Aviemore, a good trail leads through the magnificent and varied woodlands. After some clearings, the walk passes tiny but picturesque Lochan Deò, renowned for its dragonflies. In winter and spring, the snow-capped mountains often provide a stunning backdrop.

Continuing, the route eventually reaches a path that encircles the, rightly popular, Loch an Eilein. Huge old pines and younger trees fringe a beautiful stretch of water which boasts its own island castle. After leaving the loch there is the option to climb the small but prominent hill of Ord Bàn. The steep climb is rewarded by an excellent, tranquil viewpoint. The walk then crosses farmland before delving back into the woods for the return via Blackpark to the start.

ROTHIEMURCHUS FOREST & LOCH AN EILEIN

DISTANCE: 14.8KM/9.2MILES » **TOTAL ASCENT:** 311M/1,020 FT » **START GR:** NH 914106 » **TIME:** ALLOW 4.5 HOURS
SATNAV: PH22 1QN » **MAP:** OS EXPLORER 57, CAIRN GORM & AVIEMORE, 1:25,000 » **REFRESHMENTS:** SNACKS AVAILABLE
AT LOCH AN EILEIN VISITOR CENTRE ON ROUTE, OTHERWISE THE DRUIE, ROTHIEMURCHUS CENTRE » **NAVIGATION:**
STRAIGHTFORWARD EXCEPT FOR OPTIONAL ASCENT OF ORD BÀN WHICH IS ROUGH AND STEEP.

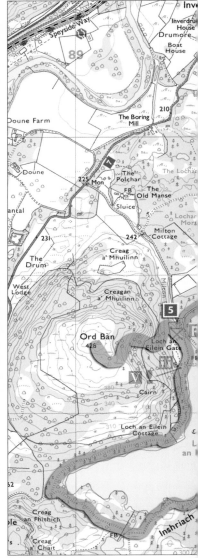

06 ROTHIEMURCHUS FOREST & LOCH AN EILEIN

Directions – Rothiemurchus Forest & Loch an Eilein

➡ There is a parking layby just before the Rothiemurchus campsite on the south side of the B970 between Inverdruie and Coylumbridge, a few kilometres south-east of Aviemore; the bus to Glenmore also stops opposite here. **Begin by taking the path** signed *Braemar via the Lairig Ghru* (next to the big road sign), and go **straight across** the cycle path on to a track. This runs alongside the woodland campsite before going through a gate and continuing past the now derelict Larig Ghru Cottage, and then through another gate.

2 At a fork **branch left** signed *Lairig Ghru* and follow the flat path onwards through the woods – here a mixture of young and old Scots pine and juniper form part of one of the largest remnants of the ancient Caledonian Forest that once covered much of Scotland. **Climb a stile** at a gate and continue ahead. Go through a gateway in an old stone wall as the track narrows and the great cleft of the Lairig Ghru eventually comes into view ahead as the trees thin out. **Bear left** at a junction for the short detour to the Cairngorm Club Footbridge. This is where the walkers' route through the Lairig Ghru to Deeside crosses the Am Beanaidh – it makes a lovely place for a stop.

  ➡ If you don't want to visit the river and bridge, **turn right** at the junction following the sign for *Loch an Eilein*.

3 Don't cross the bridge but **return back** to the junction and **bear left** signed *Loch an Eilein*. The path crosses more open ground before reaching Lochan Deò, a haven for dragonflies and damselflies. **Go straight on** at the crossroads (signed *Loch an Eilein*) and **straight ahead** again at a further junction of paths. **Bear right** where a path joins and continue through sparse pines, juniper, heather and blaeberry, crossing a burn on a footbridge.

4 **Turn left** to go through a gate when the path around Loch an Eilein is reached. Keep following the main path, **bearing right** as it skirts the loch passing a number of mature pines. Ignore the path to the left (signed *Unmaintained Path*), instead continuing to cross a footbridge; **bear right** to stay on the main path. **Keep right** where a grassy track joins from the left and soon go through a gate to pass a cottage with views to Loch an Eilein Castle, set on a tiny island to the right. **Continue ahead** at the end of the loch (turn left for Loch an Eilein visitor centre shop and toilets) to reach the car park entrance. To include Ord Bàn, **bear left** to cross the parking area aiming for the furthest corner near an old building. Pass this and **climb the awkward high stile** next to the gate, and then **bear left** on a faint path. **Branch right** at a fork and follow the faint path as it **zigzags steeply uphill**. Once out of the trees **bear right** over heather and rock to reach the wee summit with fantastic views to the Cairngorms.

↪ The ascent of Ord Bàn, which is steep and rough underfoot, can be avoided to make a shorter walk. Instead of walking through the car park just **bear right** to reach the road and continue as in point 5.

5 From the summit of Ord Bàn **return to the car park** and **keep left** to reach the road. Follow this for a short distance and then **turn right** on to a track (signed *Rothiemurchus Centre and Old Logging Way*), leading gently uphill. **Ignore a track on the right** opposite a field which often houses farmed deer (the venison is available at the Rothiemurchus Centre shop). **Continue ahead** through a gate and uphill past a cottage. Eventually two houses and the road at Blackpark are reached. **Keep straight ahead** on to the road and soon **go through a metal kissing gate on the right** and follow the path through the woods. Further on, go through a gate and the path soon emerges on to the Old Logging Way cycle route. **Turn right** here to return to the start.

CRESTED TIT

LOOKING ACROSS STRATHSPEY FROM THE LOWER SLOPES

07 Geal-charn Mòr

12.6km/7.8miles

This straightforward ascent in the Monadhliath offers classic views back over the strath to the Cairngorms.

Lynwilg » Alltnacriche gate » Burma Road Summit » Geal-charn Mòr » Balliniluig » Lynwilg

Start

Lynwilg off the A9, verge parking just over the bridge. GR: NH 882107.

The Walk

The Monadhliath mountains are often overlooked as they lack the drama of their nearby cousins on the main Cairngorm plateau. In fact these rounded hills make an excellent outdoor playground and are quieter, providing great opportunities for wildlife watching and offer some of the best views around. This relatively straight-forward route follows a track for much of the climb and is a good option for winter conditions when snowshoes or even skis can add fun to the outing for those with experience. In such conditions, or when an easier day is required, the route can be shortened, as the described descent is over rougher, wet heather.

Starting from Lynwilg the walk begins through pleasant birchwood, climbing a track beyond the woods. The route is well graded and you may well be passed by mountain bikers who like to make a challenging circuit from Aviemore taking in part of this route to Carrbridge. Known as the Burma Road, the track is thought to have been constructed in the 1940s by prisoners of war.

The high point of the Burma Road is marked with a large cairn. The walk leaves the track here to take a path over the peat and heather moorland, climbing directly to reach the rounded summit of Geal-charn Mòr. Classified as a Corbett, the summit is marked by a whitewashed trig point. This provides a fantastic panorama over Spey-side, the Cairngorm mountains and the Monadhliath. If taking the more difficult return route, the route backtracks almost to the Burma Road summit, turning sharp right before the cairn to descend a sometimes boggy and rough moorland path. There are good views down over Loch Alvie; in all but the worst weather the downhill section is enjoyable. The path emerges at Balliniluig, from where it is a short walk back to Lynwilg.

GEAL-CHARN MÒR

DISTANCE: 12.6KM/7.8MILES » **TOTAL ASCENT:** 608M/1,995FT » **START GR:** NH 882107 » **TIME:** ALLOW 4.5 HOURS **SATNAV:** PH22 1PZ » **MAPS:** OS EXPLORER 56, BADENOCH & UPPER STRATHSPEY, AND 57, CAIRN GORM & AVIEMORE, 1:25,000 » **REFRESHMENTS:** THE DRUIE, ROTHIEMURCHUS CENTRE, OR MOUNTAIN CAFE, AVIEMORE » **NAVIGATION:** STRAIGHTFORWARD ON TRACK, GOOD NAVIGATION SKILLS NEEDED ON OPEN HILL AND ROUGHER DESCENT.

07 **GEAL-CHARN MÒR**

Directions – Geal-charn Mòr

➎ Just south of Aviemore, Lynwilg is off the north side of the A9. There is limited parking just over the bridge on the right. **Start the walk by heading up the surfaced road** signed *Carrbridge via the Burma Road*. **Branch right** at a fork, following the track through trees and passing a house at Alltnacriche. There is sometimes an honesty box here with home baking – popular amongst the mountain bikers who like to take on the challenge of the Burma Road.

2 **Go through the gate** just beyond Alltnacriche and the track now steepens considerably as it climbs uphill. **Go through a further gate** and uphill on to more open ground beyond the birch trees. A few scattered pines grow nearer the water down on the left but the track is now climbing over heather moorland.

3 Eventually a large cairn marks the high point of the Burma Road. Continuing ahead here leads to Carrbridge, a popular mountain biking route. **Turn left** at the cairn and take the rough, **right hand path** uphill directly towards Geal-charn Mòr. **Continue uphill**, the path can be wet and is eroded in places but generally easy to follow. **Climb a stile** over a fence and continue towards the summit. The hill flattens off for a gentle approach to the trig point and shelter cairn.

4 For such a straightforward ascent, this peak has one of the best views around, with expansive vistas of the Cairngorm range, taking in the Feshie hills, Braeriach, Cairn Gorm and Bynack More, and looking the other way the seemingly endless Monadhliath plateau. From the summit **retrace the route back** almost to the cairn at the high point of the Burma Road. Just before the cairn and track **bear right** on to a path. **Aim diagonally half-right** (south-south-east) across the moor at first, crossing a number of small streams and staying on the faint path. At around 630m **head directly down the slope** (south-east) eventually running close to the Coachan Ruadh burn on the right.

> ▶ OR ▶ For a shorter and easier descent which avoids the boggy and rough going, retrace the outward route from the summit of Geal-charn Mòr.

5 When the field above Balliniluig is reached, **go through the farm gate** and **keep to the left** of a sheep fank to another gate. **Go through this gate** and pick up a track. **Turn left** to pass below the farmhouse at Balliniluig. Follow the track as it swings left through the farmyard and behind the steading building. The track now bends right heading towards the A9. Just before the track reaches the A9 **fork left** to go through a gate and bear left around a small hillock to join a track. **Turn right** to return to the start at Lynwilg.

THE SUMMIT

AN LOCHAN UAINE

08 Meall a' Bhuachaille & An Lochan Uaine

15.9km/9.9miles

Caledonian pines, a mysterious green lochan and a bothy add interest to this small hill with big views.

Glenmore » An Lochain Uaine » Ryvoan Bothy » Meall a' Bhuachaille » Creagan Gorm » Craiggowrie » Glenmore

Start

Glenmore Visitor Centre, Glenmore (parking charge). GR: NH 977098.

The Walk

Meall a' Bhuachaille and its neighbours lie separate from the main mass of the Cairngorms giving it views out of all proportion to the effort of the ascent. This full-day route can be shortened to a less strenuous four-hour walk if required.

Starting from the Glenmore Visitor Centre it passes a memorial to members of the Norwegian resistance who trained here during WWII before returning to fight the German occupation. Hairier Scandinavian reindeer can be encountered at the Cairngorm Reindeer Centre, also passed at the start of the walk, although you may be lucky enough to spot these lovely creatures at first hand on the hill as they roam freely on this part of the Cairngorms. A track becomes a rough path that squeezes and climbs between ancient pine trees and provides great views before descending to reach An Lochan Uaine – the green lochan. The colour is due to fairies doing their laundry in it, or mineral deposits if you are feeling more prosaic. It is a lovely spot for a quick break before following the track up to Ryvoan Bothy. Traditionally an overnight stop for walkers, it has provided vital shelter for thousands of outdoor folk over the years.

From the bothy the walking gets tougher on the steep ascent of Meall a' Bhuachaille. The path is good and pitched steps ease the climb to the huge summit cairn, a great place to look out across much of Strathspey.

A steady descent leads to a bealach and decision time – a left turn significantly shortens the route by returning directly to Glenmore, but the complete ridge walk ahead provides solitude and more expansive views over several minor summits before a longer return through the forest.

MEALL A' BHUACHAILLE & AN LOCHAN UAINE

DISTANCE: 15.9KM/9.9MILES » TOTAL ASCENT: 773M/2,536FT » START GR: NH 977098 » TIME: ALLOW 6 HOURS SATNAV: PH22 1QU » MAP: OS EXPLORER 57 CAIRN GORM & AVIEMORE, 1:25,000 » REFRESHMENTS: COBBS CAFE, GLENMORE VISITOR CENTRE » NAVIGATION: STRAIGHTFORWARD UNLESS LOW VISIBILITY OR WINTER CONDITIONS WHEN CARE IS NEEDED.

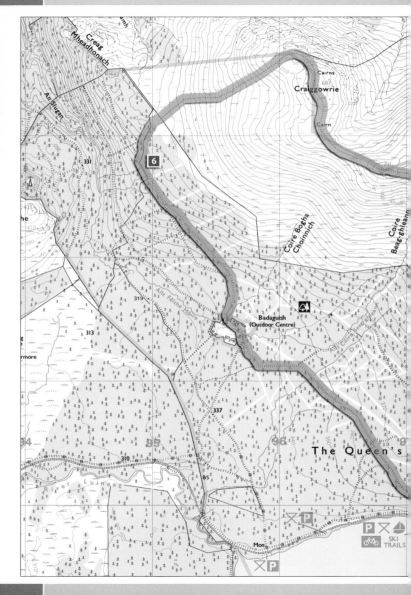

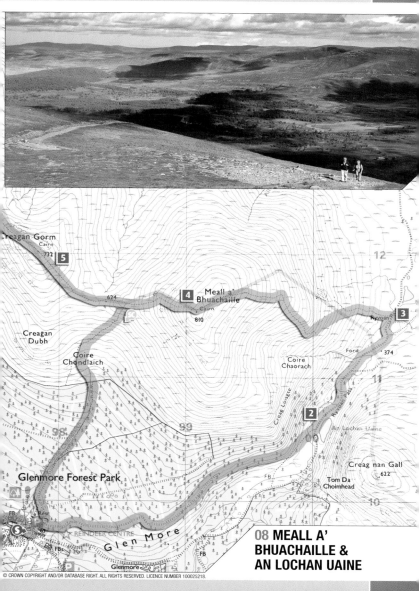

08 MEALL A' BHUACHAILLE & AN LOCHAN UAINE

Directions – Meall a' Bhuachaille & An Lochan Uaine

↱ From the car park walk up towards the Glenmore Visitor Centre (information, shop, toilets, cafe) and **keep right** of it. At the lane opposite the Cairngorm Reindeer Centre **turn left** uphill. **Branch right** at a fork, now following a forestry track. When the track ends **continue ahead** on a path which winds through the ancient pines and juniper bushes, and is rough underfoot in places. **Descend steps** and boardwalk to soon **join a larger path**.

2 **Turn left** – the green waters of An Lochan Uaine are just off the other side of the path. Head uphill on the wide path and at a junction **fork left** signed *Nethy Bridge*. There are good views over Strath Nairn, part of the RSPB's vast Abernethy National Nature Reserve. The small stone building that comes into view ahead is Ryvoan Bothy, an open shelter maintained for walkers to stay in by the Mountain Bothies Association.

3 **Turn left** at the bothy and follow the pitched path uphill. **Climb the slopes** of Meall a' Bhuachaille; the climb is steep in places but always on a good path. The summit shelter cairn is huge and provides a wonderful view across to Cairn Gorm and over Loch Morlich.

4 From the summit **take the path west** (almost directly behind you as you look to Cairn Gorm) and soon **head downhill**. At the low point, or bealach, **continue ahead** to start climbing towards Creagan Gorm.

> **↱** For a much shorter walk **turn left** at the bealach to head directly downhill to the treeline and then **follow the Allt Coire Chondlaich**. Once in the dense forestry plantation follow orange waymarkers; **turn right** to descend more steeply and emerge at the Glenmore Visitor Centre at the start.

5 The summit of Creagan Gorm at 732m is marked by a cairn. Keep an eye out for reindeer; members of the free-ranging herd are sometimes found up here. They tend to move around in small groups and will remain feeding or sometimes cooling off on snow patches on sunny days, as long as you don't try and get too close. **Continue ahead** as the path undulates along the ridge, small cairns mark the route. Beyond the summit of Craiggowrie **bear left** (south-west); the path starts to head downhill aiming for the forestry far below. The path is faint in places but easily followed with care. At the trees keep ahead on the path (now with orange waymarkers which are followed all the way back).

6 Turn left on to another path and later **continue ahead** to join a track and follow this to Badaguish. Here an outdoor centre caters for a range of visitors including those with disabilities. **Keep left** of the chalets and then **straight ahead** on the road which passes between the buildings. At an orange marker **turn left** on to a track. At a road junction **turn left** signed *Youth Hostel* and pass behind the hostel building to reach the car park at the start.

DESCENDING FROM MEALL A' BHUACHAILLE

SGÒR AN LOCHAIN UAINE FROM THE SUMMIT OF BEN MACDUI

09 Ben Macdui via the Northern Corries 16.2km/10.1miles

This superb circuit crosses the vast arctic plateau at the heart of the mountains to climb to the highest of the Cairngorms.

Cairngorm Ski Centre Car Park » Miadan Creag an Leth-choin » March Burn » Ben Macdui » Lochan Buidhe » Stob Coire an t-Sneachda » Fiacaill a' Choire Chais » Cairngorm Ski Centre Car Park

Start

Cairngorm Ski Centre car park (parking charge). GR: NH 989059.

The Walk

Once thought to be Britain's highest mountain, Ben Macdui was officially demoted to second place in 1847. This spares it the heavy foot traffic that affects Ben Nevis, keeping it as a truly remote place. The route to it is wild and exceptionally exposed to the elements – a piece of the arctic in Scotland. The high start from the end of the ski road from Glenmore makes the ascent relatively straightforward for such a big mountain, when blessed by fine summer weather. This very accessibility has led to numerous mountain rescues and some past fatalities; conditions can quickly change from a benign sunny day to a windswept white-out in minutes, with the fiercest winds imaginable. Navigation can become very difficult on the plateau so you need to be confident with map and compass work as well as properly equipped.

well-made path that also leads to Coire an t-Sneachda and Coire an Lochain. Passing the entrance to these granite bowls, a path climbs the ridge to the west of Coire an Lochain, soon venturing up into ptarmigan territory. The ridge climbs steadily before crossing a vast stony plateau. From here the route climbs once more up on to the summit plateau of Ben Macdui, its top marked by a huge cairn and trig point. On a clear day the view is exceptionally extensive, but on claggier days you may feel the presence of the Big Grey Man who is said to haunt the hill.

The descent route returns the same way initially before veering across the eastern slopes of Cairn Lochan to reach the spectacular rim of Coire an t-Sneachda. It skirts around the top of the cliffs until descending the Fiacaill a' Choire Chais ridge. Eventually a ski run is crossed and a track leads back down to the car park.

BEN MACDUI VIA THE NORTHERN CORRIES

DISTANCE: 16.2KM/10.1MILES » **TOTAL ASCENT:** 837M/2,746FT » **START GR:** NH 989059 » **TIME:** ALLOW 7.5 HOURS **SATNAV:** PH22 1RB » **MAP:** OS EXPLORER 57, CAIRN GORM & AVIEMORE, 1:25,000 » **REFRESHMENTS:** CAIRNGORM CAFE, CAIRNGORM SKI CENTRE » **NAVIGATION:** GOOD NAVIGATION SKILLS NEEDED; NAVIGATION COMPLICATED IN POOR VISIBILITY OR WINTER CONDITIONS.

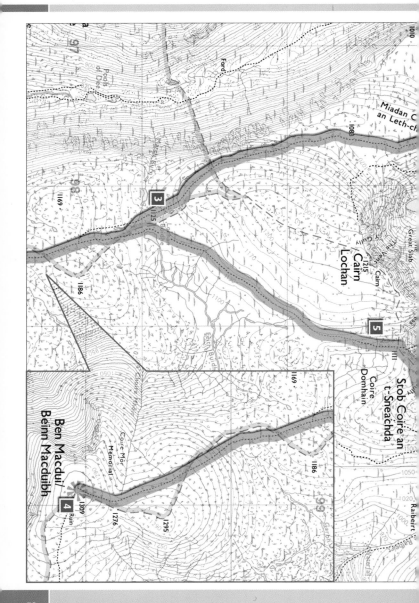

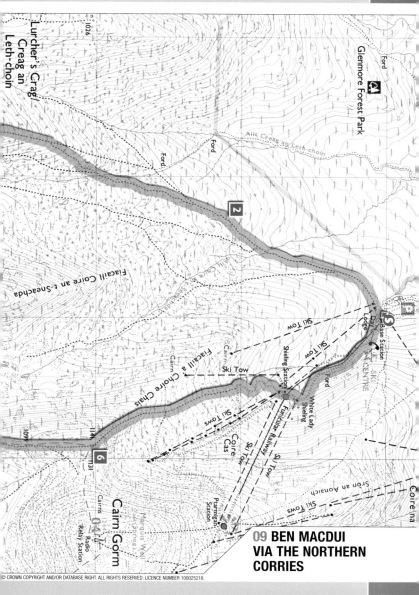

**09 BEN MACDUI
VIA THE NORTHERN
CORRIES**

Directions – Ben Macdui via the Northern Corries

➲ From the far end of the upper level of the car park **go down steps** opposite the Day Lodge, **cross a bridge and up steps** on the far side to follow a path across the moor. **Branch right** at a fork, the other path heads into Coire an t-Sneachda. Cross the moor and then **cross the Allt Coire an t-Sneachda** on giant stepping stones. **Keep right** at the next path junction, leaving behind the smaller path leading to Coire an Lochain.

2 **Start to climb** more steadily up the clear path on the broad ridge Miadan Creag an Leth-choin. The cliffs steepen as the lochan in Coire an Lochain comes into view. When the gradient eases the path leads south across flatter, stony ground. Further on the path becomes clearer once more; **aim slightly further left** to bear east-south-east to traverse the slope high above the steep ground of the Lairig Ghru. In winter conditions, it may be best to take a higher line to keep well back from this steep ground.

3 Eventually the March Burn is reached. **Keep to the right of Lochan Buidhe.** Continue **straight ahead** (south-east) crossing very stony ground and climbing gently before a short slight downhill section. **Aim half-right** (south-west) for a longer climb to reach the summit cairn marking Ben Macdui's highest point.

4 In good weather, it is worth exploring the summit plateau, with its many shelter cairns as there are some fine viewpoints. **Retrace the route** back towards Lochan Buidhe. **Branch right** to follow a path around the right-hand side of the lochan, and **bear right** to traverse the slope of Cairn Lochan.

5 Eventually the cliffs of the northern corries are reached at the bealach between Cairn Lochan and Stob Coire an t-Sneachda. **Turn right** (east-north-east), keeping well back from the edge, especially if snow corniced, to follow the dramatic cliff edge uphill. From the cairn marking the high point **continue along the edge** which gradually curves northwards, descending and then climbing for a short distance.

6 A cairn marks the top of the Fiacaill a' Choire Chais ridge. **Head north-west** to start the descent on a rocky path. The path leaves the ridge at 1,000m height, **bear right** to follow it down towards the ski runs. Eventually it emerges on a ski track, **turn left** to follow this as it zigzags all the way back to the ski centre car park at the start.

10 **Chalamain Gap Circuit**

18.1km/11.2miles

Dramatic mountain views, a rocky pass, the glacier-sculpted entrance to the Lairig Ghru, spectacular pines and lovely Loch Morlich, makes this a great introduction to the Cairngorms.

Sugarbowl Car Park, Glenmore » Utsi's Bridge » Chalamain Gap » Lairig Ghru » Piccadilly, Rothiemurchus » Loch Morlich » Allt Mòr » Sugarbowl Car Park, Glenmore

Start

Sugarbowl car park, on left-hand side of Glenmore to Cairngorm Ski Centre road (parking charge). GR: NH 984074.

The Walk

Starting from the Sugarbowl car park just below the tree line of Glenmore Forest on the road to the Cairngorm Ski Centre, the route is immediately immersed in wild nature as it leads down to the clear waters of the Allt Mòr. The bridge here is named after Mikel Utsi, a Sami reindeer herder who reintroduced the animals to the Cairngorms in 1952. Today the free-ranging herd can often be seen on the high tops, or smaller hills such as nearby Meall a' Bhuachaille; and you may see some in enclosed paddocks on this walk.

The route follows clear paths across open ground with vast forests below and the craggy northern corries above, aiming for the Chalamain Gap, a dramatic deep cleft,

to gain access to the next glen. The floor of the gap is strewn with boulders and passing through it involves rock hopping, needing care and agility. On the far side a path leads down into the equally dramatic but far grander u-shaped trough of the Lairig Ghru, the traditional and challenging foot pass through the Cairngorms, linking Deeside and Braemar.

This route turns right away from the pass, following the Allt Druidh to reach the tree line – one of the most beautiful places in the whole of the Cairngorms National Park. A path leads down through twisted old granny pines before reaching the shores of Loch Morlich. This celebrated loch enjoys a magnificent setting and well deserves its popularity. The route follows tracks south of the loch, before a final stretch alongside the Allt Mòr leads back to Utsi's Bridge and the return to the start.

CHALAMAIN GAP CIRCUIT

DISTANCE: 18.1KM/11.2MILES » **TOTAL ASCENT:** 510M/1,673FT » **START GR:** NH 984074 » **TIME:** ALLOW 7 HOURS **SATNAV:** PH22 1RB » **MAP:** OS EXPLORER 57, CAIRN GORM & AVIEMORE, 1:25,000 » **REFRESHMENTS:** NONE ON ROUTE, NEAREST IS COBBS CAFE, GLENMORE VISITOR CENTRE » **NAVIGATION:** STRAIGHTFORWARD; CHALAMAIN GAP CAN BE HAZARDOUS IN SNOW.

REINDEER

10 CHALAMAIN GAP CIRCUIT

Directions – Chalamain Gap Circuit

⑤ From the car park take the path **slightly uphill** from the information board to reach the road. **Cross the road** and take the path on the far side which **heads downhill** to reach Utsi's Bridge over the Allt Mòr. **Cross the bridge** and climb the steep path to reach the top of a high bank. Ahead are the private paddocks often used for guided visits to see the Cairngorm reindeer herd. **Bear left** to follow the top of the high bank. The path crosses open ground with great views ahead to Cairn Gorm and her northern corries.

2 Eventually descend gently to **cross the Caochan Dubh a' Chadha**. Keep **straight ahead** where a rough path leaves to the right. The rocky cleft of the Chalamain Gap can now be seen ahead.

3 The route through the Chalamain Gap stays close to the bottom of the pass but involves clambering over numerous boulders. It lies between Creag a' Chalamain and Lurcher's Crag and provides an atmospheric, although often very windy, arrival on the far side where the mountain of Braeriach can be seen directly ahead. **Keep straight ahead** as the path descends gently at first and then more steeply to reach the Allt Druidh.

> ▷OR▷ Chalamain Gap has been the site of fatal avalanches so in some snowy conditions the safest option will be to **aim half-right** before the gap to head south-west to gain the summit of Creag a' Chalamain before **bearing left** to head south to regain the path on the far side of the gap.

4 The Lairig Ghru, the eventual gateway to Deeside, is the prominent glacial-carved deep glen to the left. **Turn right** at the water to follow the clear path which heads away from the mountains towards the forest of Rothiemurchus. **Fork left** at a junction (the right fork leads to Rothiemurchus Lodge, regularly used by the armed forces as a training base) to stay high above the Allt Druidh passing some spectacular old pine trees and younger regenerating woodland.

5 Eventually, at the end of the descent, the path junction known as Piccadilly is reached. **Turn right** here and stay on the main path to pass the wildlife rich woods. At a junction with a track from the right **keep straight on** to follow this track soon passing Lochan nan Geadas.

6 **Turn right** at the next junction to skirt the southern shore of Loch Morlich on a forestry track. **Continue straight ahead** ignoring some tracks to the right and a waymarked path to the left. Eventually the track descends to the Glenmore road near the Hayfield car park.

7 **Cross the road** and follow a narrow path **straight ahead**. At a bigger path **turn right** to follow this slightly uphill. **Continue ahead** across a track to reach the Allt Mòr car park. **Keep straight on** and cross the footbridge over the Allt Mòr. Immediately **turn right** and follow the burn and then a series of boardwalks. When the road is reached go **diagonally across** and take a delightful path which shadows the water upstream crossing a couple of footbridges before reaching the outward route at Utsi's Bridge. **Turn left** here to take the path uphill back to the road and the Sugarbowl car park at the start.

THE CHALAMAIN GAP

CAIRN GORM & THE SRÒN A' CHA-NO RIDGE

DISTANCE: 12.2KM/7.6MILES » **TOTAL ASCENT:** 783M/2,569FT » **START GR:** NH 989059 » **TIME:** ALLOW 6 HOURS
SATNAV: PH22 1RB » **MAP:** OS EXPLORER 57, CAIRN GORM & AVIEMORE, 1:25,000 » **REFRESHMENTS:** CAIRNGORM CAFE,
CAIRNGORM SKI CENTRE » **NAVIGATION:** GOOD NAVIGATION SKILLS NEEDED FOR DESCENT SECTION ON PATHLESS GROUND,
NAVIGATION COMPLICATED IN POOR VISIBILITY OR WINTER CONDITIONS.

DISTANT BEN NEVIS SEEN FROM CAIRN GORM

11 Cairn Gorm & the Sròn a' Cha-no Ridge

12.2km/7.6miles

Get a different perspective on this popular high mountain.

Cairngorm Ski Centre Car Park » Windy Ridge Path » Ptarmigan Station » Cairn Gorm Summit » Cnap Coire na Spreidhe » Sròn a' Cha-no » Lochan na Beinne » Coire na Ciste Car Park » Cairngorm Ski Centre Car Park

Start

Cairngorm Ski Centre car park (parking charge). GR: NH 989059.

The Walk

Cairn Gorm is the best-known mountain in the region, giving its name to the range and dominating the landscape around Glenmore. This walk ascends it via the main Windy Ridge Path, climbing through the ugly ski developments before reaching the summit and its vast panoramas. The return route provides a completely different perspective on the mountain; the wild north ridge is largely pathless and little visited, providing much more challenging going. This is a great place to seek real solitude, where mountain hares and ptarmigan may be your only companions. If you don't fancy the wilder descent, you can simply retrace your steps.

The well-constructed Windy Ridge Path climbs away from the ski buildings and other paraphernalia. The climb is steady but never too strenuous and the path continues, crossing a ski run at one point, to reach the large Ptarmigan Station building. Continuing upwards from here the route follows a pitched path and then cairns all the way to the summit. Here a meteorological station automatically records the extremes of mountain weather, which is subject to arctic conditions. The strongest wind recorded here was a gust of 173mph in 1986; even on a seemingly benign weather day, conditions can vary wildly from those experienced down at the car park.

In good conditions the return route is a pathless delight. It heads across bouldery terrain to reach the outlying top of Cnap Coire na Spreidhe, and then descends down the broad north ridge. This is a very different side of the mountain, retaining its wild beauty. Walking down from arctic tundra conditions to reach what would be the natural treeline, sections of rough path pass an attractive lochan and the fast flowing Allt na Ciste before reaching the Coire na Ciste car park. From here a short uphill section of road walking is required to return to the start.

Directions – Cairn Gorm & the Sròn a' Cha-no Ridge

➎ From the main car park at Coire Cas **head uphill** on the track between the funicular building and the Day Lodge. Almost immediately **turn left** on to a path signed *Windy Ridge*. This stone-pitched path climbs steadily, the ever-increasing views behind provide a good excuse for stops. As height is gained the gradient on the broad ridge eases. Keep on the path, at one point crossing a ski run, and soon the Ptarmigan Station is reached.

2 **Keep to the left** of the Ptarmigan Station and pass behind it. From here take the pitched footpath to **climb steeply south** between wooden posts. The wind can often be ferocious as the route reaches much higher and exposed ground. Beyond the wooden posts the path becomes rougher and stonier, a series of large cairns marks the route. **Keep straight ahead** (south) to reach the summit cairn and the nearby weather station building which in winter is often festooned with huge wind-blown icicles.

3 From the summit **bear north-east** at first, aiming for the low point between Cairn Gorm and Cnap Coire na Spreidhe. From here follow the easy ground, **climb gently east** to reach this top. Good views open up into the steep cleft of Strath Nethy down to the right.

4 From the summit **follow the broad ridge downhill north at first** and then **aim north-east** to reach the spot height of 1,028m above Coire Laogh Mòr. From here the ridge is much more defined and easier to follow, there is now a faint path on the ground. **Continue downhill,** aiming north to follow the ridge of Sròn a' Cha-no. Eventually there is a steeper descent to a small bealach.

5 At this low point and before the ridge starts to climb, **turn west** to leave the ridge and continue the descent. **Aim towards the southern end of Lochan na Beinne;** there is a rough path. The path soon **crosses a stream;** careful navigation is needed on the next stretch as there are several paths crossing the moor, which is boggy in places. There is a clearer path as the route nears and crosses the Allt na Ciste. **Climb up steps** to reach the Coire na Ciste car park.

6 Once a popular ski area, the Ciste has been disused for many years. **Head straight across** the car park and **keep left** to take the upper section of road and walk back uphill. At the road junction **turn left** to return to the Cairngorm Ski Centre car park and the start.

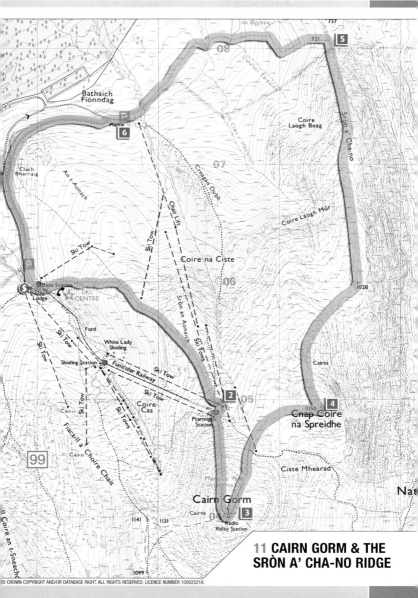

11 CAIRN GORM & THE SRÒN A' CHA-NO RIDGE

BREARIACH FROM WHITEWELL

DISTANCE: 26.5KM/16.5MILES » **TOTAL ASCENT:** 1,217M/3,993FT » **START GR:** NH 915087 » **TIME:** ALLOW 10 HOURS » **SATNAV:** PH22 1QT » **MAP:** OS EXPLORER 57, CAIRN GORM & AVIEMORE, 1:25,000 » **REFRESHMENTS:** NONE ON ROUTE, NEAREST IS THE DRUIE, ROTHIEMURCHUS CENTRE » **NAVIGATION:** GOOD MAP-READING SKILLS REQUIRED, SUMMIT PLATEAU DIFFICULT TO NAVIGATE AND DANGEROUS IN POOR WEATHER.

SRÒN NA LAIRIGE, SEEN FROM THE STRATH

12 Braeriach from Whitewell

26.5km/16.5miles

Remote Braeriach is Britain's third highest mountain and amongst its wildest and grandest.

Whitewell » Cairngorm Club Footbridge » Lairig Ghru » Sròn na Lairige » Braeriach Summit » Braeriach NW flank » Am Beanaidh » Lochan Deò » Whitewell

Start

Whitewell parking area reached by minor road from Inverdruie, south-west of Aviemore (signed *Blackpark*). GR: NH 915087.

The Walk

This route provides a taste of everything that makes the Cairngorms so special; a long approach through beautiful pinewoods, a vast plateau exposed to the elements, magnificent craggy corries, a spectacular high summit and a genuine sense of remote wildness. It's a challenging day requiring a fair amount of hill experience.

The most usual ascent of Braeriach is from the Sugarbowl car park at Glenmore, but this route from Whitewell makes a much finer outing, gradually climbing up through the natural treeline into the deep cleft of the Lairig Ghru on the approach, and making a return possible via Gleann Eanaich.

Once over the Cairngorm Club Footbridge the walk rises through the gnarly ancient Caledonian pines, crossing the treeline into the mouth of the Lairig Ghru. It then heads on to a broad ridge with dramatic views over the glacial trench, fringed by cliffs, with Lurcher's Crag impressive across the void.

After crossing the minor summit of Sròn na Lairige, a short descent leads to a narrow neck before the climb up to the summit around the dramatic high and jagged cliffs of Coire Bhrochain. The cairn at 1,296 metres is the third highest summit in the UK, and offers stunning views across the remote and spectacular An Garbh Choire.

From the top a short section of rocky plateau leads to the cliffs of secretive Coire an Lochain, named for the small loch nestled within the deep bowl far below. The route now descends the rocky and steep north-west flank of the mountain; a stalker's path makes the descent less daunting than it might look but your knees will still feel it. Once down in Gleann Eanaich the route follows a track alongside the waters of the Am Beanaidh, fording a side burn lower down. The return to the forests of Rothiemurchus feels like coming home, as the route heads back to Whitewell.

Directions – Braeriach from Whitewell

➡ Park at the small parking area on the left-hand side, near the end of the public road at Whitewell; take the path **downhill** (signed *Rothiemurchus*) from just before the parking. At a junction with a larger path **turn right**. Braeriach and the Lairig Ghru can be seen in the distance. At a crosspaths **turn left** and pass Lochan Deò, a lovely small loch nestled in the pine trees. **Keep right** when a path coming in from Coylumbridge joins from the left (an alternative start point).

2 At the Am Beanaidh river **cross the iron bridge** built over 100 years ago by the Cairngorm Club, the oldest Scottish hillwalking club – it was founded in 1887 and is still going strong. **Bear right** on the far side and after 1km **turn right** at a crosspaths, now heading directly towards the Lairig Ghru. The path climbs beyond the natural treeline above the Allt Druidh. After a further 2km the path begins to run alongside the burn. It is soon joined by the path from the Chalamain Gap coming down on the left; shortly afterwards **cross the burn** and start to climb gently.

3 A short distance further **fork right** on to a clear path which starts to climb the lower end of the Sròn na Lairige ridge. As height is gained there are great views into the cleft of the Lairig Ghru and across the pass to the prow of Lurcher's Crag.

BRAERIACH SUMMIT

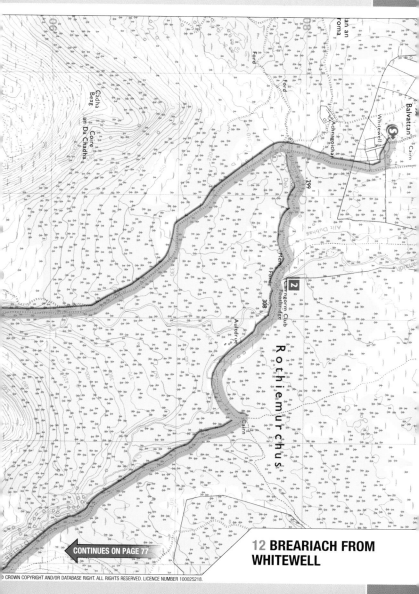

CONTINUES ON PAGE 77

12 BREARIACH FROM WHITEWELL

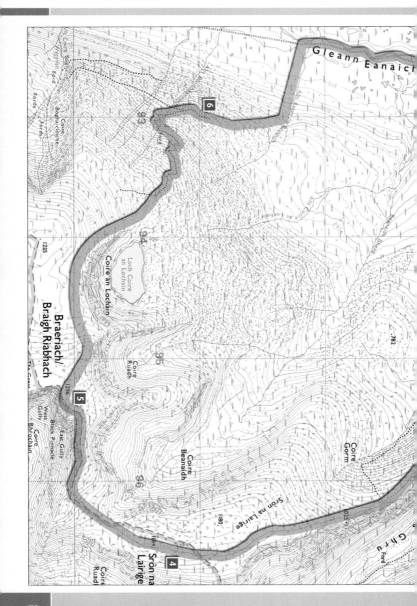

Gleann Eanaich

Coire Bogha-cloiche

Braeriach/ Braigh Riabhach

Coire an Lochain

Loch Coire an Lochain

Coire Ruadh

West Gully

Black Pinnacle

East Gully

Coire Bhrochain

Coire Ruadh

Coire Beanaidh

Sròn na Làirige

Sròn na Làirige

Coire Gorm

Allt Coire an Lochain

1235

1276

782

1180

1184

1025

6

5

4

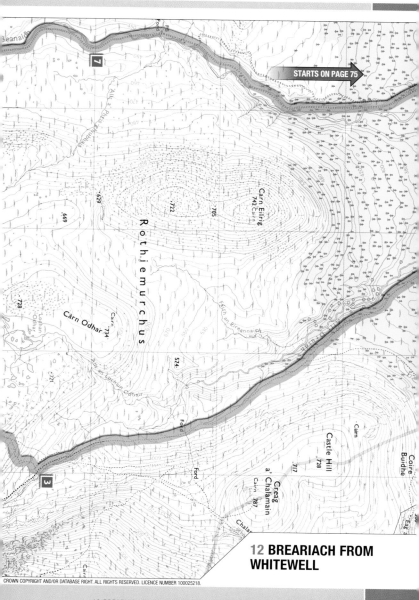

STARTS ON PAGE 75

7

Allt a' Phubbuill

Allt a' Phubbuill

·629

·669

·722

·705

Càrn Eilrig
742 Cairn

R o t h i e m u r c h u s

·728

Lochan Odhar

Càrn Odhar

Càrn
·734

Feith an Eireannaich

·574

·721

Allt an Lochain Odhair

Ford

Ford

Ford

3

Cairn

Castle Hill
·728

Coire
Buidhe

·717

Creag
a' Chalamain
Càrn 787

Coire
Eas

Chalan

12 BREARIACH FROM WHITEWELL

4 Eventually the flat top of Sròn na Lairige is reached; the summit itself can be bypassed. From here **descend half-right** (south-west) to reach the bealach and **continue** in the same direction up the slope ahead. As the ridge narrows and the route reaches the top of the steep cliffs of Coire Bhrochain **bear right** to head west-north-west along the top of the jagged cliffs. Here the views are breathtaking looking across the corrie to the peaks of Cairn Toul and Sgòr an Lochain Uaine at the very heart of the Cairngorms.

5 A short rocky gentle climb reaches the dramatic summit of Braeriach at 1,296m, very close to the cliff edge. The return route includes a crossing of the summit plateau and steep descent into Gleann Eanaich: in poor weather conditions it may be wise to retrace the outward route. If continuing the circuit **bear north-west** from the summit to reach the rim of Coire Ruadh. **Bear left** to aim west, passing above the steep cliffs of Coire an Lochain with its sizeable loch far below. **Continue descending** following the edge of the corrie aiming north-west-north until level with the bottom of the corrie. At this point **bear half-left** to aim north-west to join the remains of an old stalker's path. This path is a real boon for the descent as it heads downhill in a series of zigzags that make light work of the steep gradient so the views across Gleann Eanaich can be enjoyed.

6 When the path peters out **aim half-right** to bear north-north-east towards the Allt Easan na Bruaich. This avoids some tedious steep heather on the slopes directly ahead. **Turn left** before the stream is reached and **descend directly** into Gleann Eanaich. **Turn right** in the bottom of the glen to follow the path north. **Cross the Beanaidh Bheag** at the ford; in spate conditions this can be impassable – it often requires a shallow wade.

7 **Continue ahead** and further down the glen cross the bridge over the Am Beanaidh. **Branch right** to stay on the lower track at a fork and soon the pines of Rothiemurchus are reached. This beautiful section of glen has some lovely trees and is a haven for wildlife. At a crosspaths **go straight ahead** retracing the outward route. After another 1km **turn left** on to the path that heads back to the parking area at Whitewell.

SECTION 3

Grantown-on-Spey & Tomintoul

The elegant buildings of Grantown-on-Spey, Strathspey's capital, make a great base for exploring the wildlife-rich woodlands that surround this part of the River Spey, which is legendary for its salmon fishing. South-east of Grantown-on-Spey is the highest village in the Cairngorms National Park, Tomintoul; the gateway to the rolling moorland of the Glenlivet hills. With clear rivers, rolling farmland and moors, renowned whisky distilleries and ruined castles, this is a great area to discover on foot; a chance to get off the beaten track on walks that see fewer visitors.

THE CAIRNGORMS SEEN FROM THE DREGGIE, ABOVE GRANTOWN-ON-SPEY

THE RIVER SPEY AT GRANTOWN-ON-SPEY

13 Anagach Woods & the River Spey 11.5km/7.1miles

Explore wildlife-rich woodlands and the banks of the River Spey on this easy-going circuit.

Grantown-on-Spey » General Wade's Military Road » Speybank » Craigroy » Cromdale Bridge » Anagach Woods » Grantown-on-Spey

Start

Burnfield Avenue car park, Grantown-on-Spey, north end of High Street. GR: NJ 034280.

The Walk

Strathspey's capital is the historic planned town of Grantown-on-Spey. With its leafy square and stone-built High Street, it's been popular with visitors since Victorian times. Grantown-on-Spey makes an excellent base for wildlife and walking holidays, and is an essential stopping point on the Speyside Way long distance walk that starts at Buckie on the Moray coast.

Grantown-on-Spey is fortunate to be almost completely encircled by fine native wood-lands, especially Anagach Woods which extend for miles alongside the beautiful River Spey. The walk leads out of town along a section of one of General Wade's Military Roads constructed as part of an effort by the British Government to bring the Highlands under its control following the Jacobite rebellion of 1715.

This was part of a road which linked Dunkeld to Fort George near Inverness. A riverside path then follows the banks of the Spey, passing the fine Old Spey Bridge. A track continues along the riverbank, popular with fly fishermen in the summer months, before the route continues higher above the river.

Before reaching picturesque Cromdale Kirk and bridge, the walk turns back into the woods for the return leg, following part of the Speyside Way. This path leads deep into the heart of the woods, home to the rare – and extremely shy – capercaillie. The largest member of the grouse family, this turkey-sized bird is critically endangered; its Gaelic name means the 'horse of the woods', referring to the 'clip-clop' sound of its call. The presence of these and other ground nesting birds here means that dogs need to be kept on leads from April to August. The route passes a curling pond and golf course as it returns to the edge of Grantown-on-Spey.

ANAGACH WOODS & THE RIVER SPEY

DISTANCE: 11.5KM/7.1MILES » **TOTAL ASCENT:** 83M/272FT » **START GR:** NJ 034280 » **TIME:** ALLOW 4 HOURS **SATNAV:** PH26 3HH » **MAP:** OS EXPLORER 61, GRANTOWN-ON-SPEY & HILLS OF CROMDALE, 1:25,000 » **REFRESHMENTS:** THE HIGH STREET MERCHANTS, GRANTOWN-ON-SPEY » **NAVIGATION:** STRAIGHTFORWARD, MOSTLY MARKED PATHS.

CROMDALE KIRK ACROSS THE RIVER SPEY

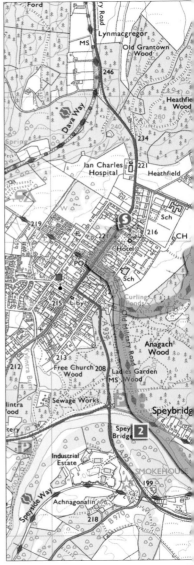

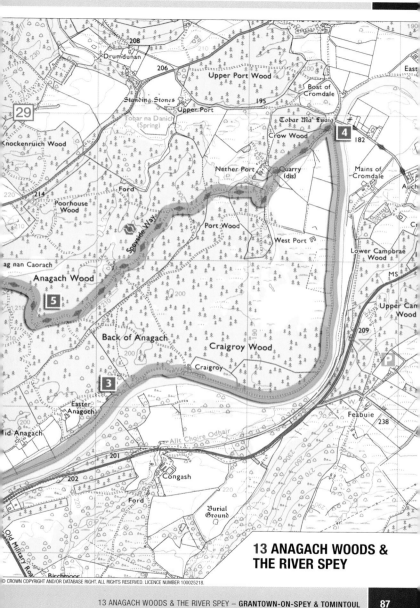

Directions – Anagach Woods & the River Spey

⑤ From the car park on Burnfield Avenue walk up to the High Street and **turn left,** soon passing the impressive Grant Arms Hotel and through the grassy 'square'. At the traffic lights at the far end of the square **turn left** on to Forest Road. At the crossroads (fire station on the right) **go straight across,** with views of the golf course on the left. **Bear right** slightly, to pass some bungalows on the right. Go through a gateway and keep **straight on** to follow the course of the Old Military Road. At the edge of the woods **continue ahead** through a small parking area, **cross the road and down steps** to reach the river bank.

2 **Turn left** to follow the path alongside the Spey. A popular salmon fishing river, ospreys also try their luck here in the summer; there are a number of nesting pairs in Strathspey. Pass under the three-span stone bridge completed in 1754 as part of the military road. If the water is very high you may have to detour up steps to cross the bridge rather than passing beneath it. Otherwise **continue ahead** to pick up a track that follows the river downstream.

3 When the track ends **continue ahead** on a narrow path which soon climbs up to join another track. **Turn right** here and soon **branch right** at a fork and go through the farm gate leading to Craigroy. **Take the path** on the right, **through a small gate and downhill** to rejoin the riverbank. The path widens to become a track, heads through a short section of dense forestry, passes a fishing hut and eventually approaches Cromdale with the iron bridge and old kirk visible ahead.

4 Before reaching these, and immediately after a gate, **turn sharp left** to double back on to a path that is part of the Speyside Way (thistle waymarker posts are followed from this point back to Grantown-on-Spey). After a metal gate **bear left** on a track, over a small bridge and soon go **straight ahead** through another gate back into the woods. The path climbs gently and then levels to head through the trees. **Keep ahead on the path** at the next two junctions, following the Speyside Way markers.

5 **Keep straight ahead** when a path comes in from the left and eventually at a more open junction **bear right**. Just before a gate leading to the golf course **turn left** on to a path which undulates and then passes through a large clearing in the woods. **Keep straight on** here; soon the path bears right back into the trees, passing the town's curling rink on the right. Keep **straight ahead** past a small parking area and finally when the outward route is rejoined **turn right** on to Forest Road to retrace your steps back to the start.

RED SQUIRREL

DESCENT FROM CARN DAIMH

14 Carn Daimh from Tomnavoulin

10.2km/6.3miles

The rolling moors of the Glenlivet Estate are the setting for this superb circuit with panoramic views.

Tomnavoulin » Westertown » Cairn Ellick Forestry » Carn Daimh » Speyside Way » Clash Wood » Tomnavoulin

Start

Car park at Clash Wood, north-west of Tomnavoulin. GR: NJ 208264.

The Walk

The hills around Glenlivet and Tomintoul – the eastern foothills of the Cairngorms – provide a more intimate, rolling countryside of farmland and grouse moors that contrast starkly with the great mountains to the west. Numerous distilleries dot the landscape; the area was once a centre of whisky smuggling. It is a remote area, subject to heavy snowfalls that can leave communities cut off in winter. This route lies within the Glenlivet Estate, starting from the tiny settlement of Tomnavoulin where a distillery now produces whisky on the site of an old carding mill, where farmers once brought fleeces to be made into wool.

The walk tracks around the edge of Clash Wood before taking old farm tracks into the hills, passing a number of disused buildings that are testament to the much larger populations that once eked out a living from the land. After a section of forestry the open moors are reached and a broad ridge is followed to the summit of Carn Daimh, a great vantage point over the surrounding countryside. The summit is a good place for a picnic lunch stop, and is popular with mountain bikers from the nearby trail centre as well as walkers on a spur of the Speyside Way.

Once away from the summit you'll likely soon find solitude once more. The unimproved grasslands lower down are a great habitat for wading birds in the spring. Listen for the calls of curlew, lapwing and oystercatchers. Once back down in Tomnavoulin the nearest and most authentic refreshment would be a dram at the Glenlivet Distillery a short distance down the glen: it has a visitor centre and cafe. Alternatively, in the opposite direction is Tomintoul, one of the highest villages in Scotland.

CARN DAIMH FROM TOMNAVOULIN

DISTANCE: 10.2KM/6.3MILES » **TOTAL ASCENT:** 339M/1,112FT » **START GR:** NJ 208264 » **TIME:** ALLOW 4 HOURS **SATNAV:** AB37 9JA » **MAP:** OS EXPLORER 61, GRANTOWN-ON-SPEY & HILLS OF CROMDALE, 1:25,000 » **REFRESHMENTS:** THE OLD MALTINGS COFFEE SHOP, GLENLIVET DISTILLERY, GLENLIVET » **NAVIGATION:** STRAIGHTFORWARD HILLWALK, PARTIALLY WAYMARKED.

Directions – Carn Daimh from Tomnavoulin

➤ From the car park **take the track leading into the woods** next to the information board waymarked in blue and white. Soon **turn left** on to a path downhill through the trees and then along the edge of Clash Wood. When a pair of gates are reached go over the two stiles and keep straight on, taking the **left fork** of the two diverging tracks ahead. **Continue ahead** and further on ignore a track on the left and pass the farm buildings at Westertown.

2 After the farm buildings **stay on the track** as it bends left and then right, using the bridge to cross the stream and continuing uphill. At a gate the track becomes much fainter, climb the stile here and keep heading uphill between fences on a grassy path. Looking back, the mountain of Ben Rinnes dominates the view. **Keep straight ahead,** going through two gates and then **cross a stile** at the end of the fence. As the path nears the forestry plantation, **go through a gate** and follow the edge of the trees until the path aims **slightly right** to head into Cairn Ellick forestry.

3 At a junction **turn right** signed *Ballindalloch*, now following a spur of the Speyside Way which links to Tomintoul (thistle waymarkers). This section can be boggy underfoot. Still in the trees, ignore a track to the left, eventually going through a gate to emerge in open countryside. **Stay on the track** as it follows a wide ridge to climb to the summit of Carn Daimh.

4 The view is excellent, and an indicator helps to identify the hills all around. Keep on the same side of the fence and **bear right** to continue on the Speyside Way, following the fence slightly downhill to approach another forestry plantation. **Continue straight ahead** at a junction. At the end of the trees **bear right** aiming for a gate. Don't go through the gate – leave the Speyside Way here and **turn right** to follow a fence.

5 **Branch left** at a fork staying close to the fence downhill with views to Glenlivet. **Turn left** over a stile and follow the path **bearing half-right downhill**. Go through a gate in a fence and **continue ahead** to a track near the woods. **Continue ahead on the track** alongside the trees. Ignore a track on the left, go through the woods to return to the car park.

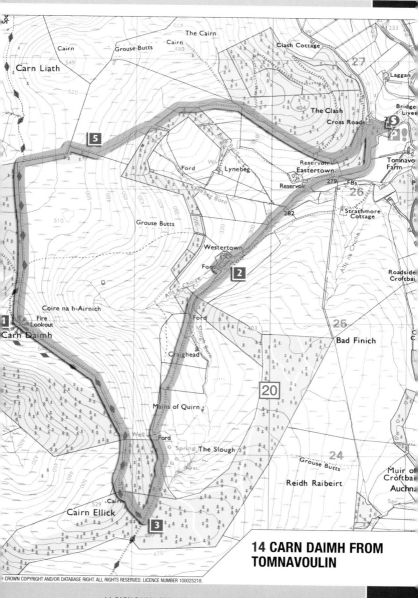

14 CARN DAIMH FROM TOMNAVOULIN

GLEN LOIN

15 Inchrory & Strath Avon

29.6km/18.4miles

This long riverside and moorland expedition has a very remote feel.

Queen's Viewpoint » Dalestie » Inchrory » Bridge over Avon » Drum Loin » Cnap Chaochan Aitinn » Carn an t-Sleibhe » Auchnahyle Bridge » Queen's Viewpoint

Start

Queen's Viewpoint car park, on left-hand side of minor road, south-west of Tomintoul. GR: NJ 164176.

The Walk

Strath Avon (pronounced *a'an*) is a long and remote glen that penetrates far into the Cairngorms from Tomintoul. The glen itself is beautiful with several areas of woodland, but the hills around it are bare. These vast areas of close-cropped heather moorland are largely a result of management for grouse shooting. Left to its natural state, and without the contributory factor of heavy grazing by deer and sheep, trees would grow higher up these hills and their summits would be clothed with montane scrub, a mix of hardy willow, juniper and other low-growing species which would compete with the heather to provide a more diverse habitat.

Near the start, the route passes a viewpoint admired by Queen Victoria who visited on one of her many pony expeditions from Balmoral. Her two-day route undertaken in 1860 saw her head from Balmoral to Grantown-on-Spey via Deeside and Glen Feshie, returning through Tomintoul and Strath Avon the following day.

The walk up the glen is long but easy, passing Inchrory and then the picturesque rapids at the Linn of Avon. At Inverloin the Avon is left behind for the return leg over the rolling grouse moors. The route crosses some pathless ground and climbs to the summit of Cnap Chaochan Aitinn before eventually returning down tracks to Strath Avon.

INCHRORY & STRATH AVON

DISTANCE: 29.6KM/18.4MILES » **TOTAL ASCENT:** 784M/2,572FT » **START GR:** NJ 164176 » **TIME:** ALLOW 8.5 HOURS **SATNAV:** AB37 9HT » **MAP:** OS EXPLORER 58, BRAEMAR, TOMINTOUL & GLEN AVON, 1:25,000 » **REFRESHMENTS:** WHISKY CASTLE CAFE OR THE GLENAVON, TOMINTOUL » **NAVIGATION:** LONG AND REMOTE ROUTE BUT MOSTLY GOOD UNDERFOOT, PATHLESS MOORLAND SECTION, THE LOIN BURN MAY BE IMPASSABLE IN SPATE.

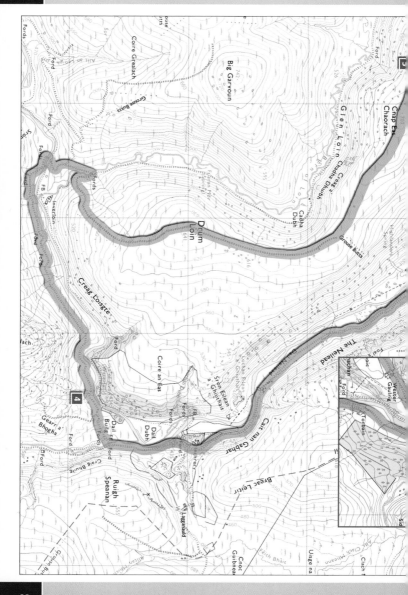

15 INCHRORY &
STRATH AVON

Directions – Inchrory & Strath Avon

➤ Take the **track at the far end of the car park**, soon going through a gate. **Turn left** to detour up steps signed *Queen's Viewpoint*. Return to the track, **turn left** and **keep left** further on at a fork near a cottage. Ahead the tors can be made out on distant Ben Avon. The track heads downhill to join the surfaced road.

2 **Continue ahead** on the road up the increasingly remote Strath Avon. At Birchfield go **straight on** through the gate. The route heads through a few stretches of woodland and passes the bridge below Auchnahyle which is used on the return walk. Pass the buildings at Torbain to continue beside the River Avon.

3 **Cross the bridge** over the Burn of Little Fergie and **head uphill** to pass the semi-ruined house at Dalestie. The track continues up the glen, keeping close to the river. Approaching the shooting lodge at Inchrory, **branch left** when the track forks to keep above the buildings. Head downhill on the track to **cross the bridge** over the Builg Burn. **Keep straight ahead**, ignoring a track to the left.

4 Soon there are views to the waterfalls known as the Linn of Avon over to the right – a good place for a break. The track climbs briefly and then heads downhill into the upper part of the glen. **Cross the bridge** over the Avon and stay on the track as it twists left and right. **Turn right** at the junction to **cross at the ford** over the Burn of Loin. **Turn right** to climb up the slopes to the top of Drum Loin. Eventually the track ends at a turning area; **continue ahead** along the now pathless ridge.

5 Pass a couple of large rocks to eventually reach the summit of Cnap Chaochan Aitinn, which is marked with a cairn and some masts. It makes a good viewpoint to Ben Rinnes and over Moray. **Take the track ahead** to aim north-west down the hill and **turn right** at a junction. At the next junction, with a shooting hut just over on the right, **turn left** to follow the track across Carn an t-Sleibhe.

6 Continue down to the Allt Bheithachan and **bear right** at the junction to follow the wooded glen. Pass Bailechnoic and Wester Gaulrig to eventually **cross to the iron bridge** below Auchnahyle. **Turn left** and retrace the outward route past Birchfield, **forking right** to once more pass the Queen's Viewpoint and return to the car park.

SECTION 4

Braemar & Deeside

To the south-east the main ranges of the Cairngorms descend to Deeside, where the sparkling River Dee threads a winding route through magnificent pinewoods. The village of Braemar is the perfect base for excursions into the Cairngorms which appear as individual hills on this approach, rather than the great wall that dominates Strathspey.

Further down the valley the Dee flows past Balmoral Castle to reach the handsome granite-built town of Ballater, and the Muir of Dinnet National Nature Reserve beyond. To the south is the Mounth, a range of plateaux almost as extensive as the Cairngorms themselves, presided over by dark Lochnagar.

LOCHNAGAR FROM THE OLD MILITARY ROAD

LOCH KINORD

16 **The Muir of Dinnet & the Vat Burn** 15.7km/9.8miles

This varied walk explores the Muir of Dinnet National Nature Reserve, with pinewoods, birchwoods, a fine loch and the spectacular rock feature of The Vat.

Burn O' Vat Visitor Centre » Vat Burn » Queel Burn » Cambus O' May Suspension Bridge » Deeside Way » Dinnet » Loch Kinord » Burn O' Vat Visitor Centre

Start

Burn O' Vat Visitor Centre, B9119, five kilometres north-east of Ballater. GR: NO 429996.

The Walk

Experience at first hand the awesome power of water, rock and ice as stepping stones lead through the narrow entrance of The Vat. This impressive bowl was carved by huge swirling rocks at a time when meltwater from the end of the last ice age was forcing its way downriver. Since it was formed it has partly filled with gravel and other debris washed downstream. Standing inside, dwarfed by the high walls of The Vat, it is hard to believe that there may well be an equal amount of spherical carved rock space beneath your feet as you can see above ground.

From The Vat the walk meanders up through the woodland before crossing a low pass and descending to the forest lochans and trails at the Cambus O' May. Here mighty Scots pine tower above pools of water providing a home for dragonflies, damselflies and the very rare pearl-bordered fritillary butterfly. The presence of ground-nesting birds including capercaillie and black grouse here means that dogs need to be kept on leads from April to August.

After crossing the A93 the route follows a cycle path on the line of the old Royal Deeside Railway, alongside the mighty River Dee at times. The beautiful old iron Cambus O' May Suspension Bridge provides a focal point before a very straight section of old railway is enlivened by the extensive birch and aspen habitat it crosses. There is a hotel offering a coffee stop or meals at the small settlement of Dinnet. Beyond this the route leads to Loch Kinord, a beautiful and tranquil body of water and home to a variety of birds.

THE MUIR OF DINNET & THE VAT BURN

DISTANCE: 15.7KM/9.8MILES » **TOTAL ASCENT:** 171M/561FT » **START** GR: NO 429996 » **TIME:** ALLOW 4.5 HOURS **SATNAV:** AB34 5NB » **MAP:** OS EXPLORER 59, ABOYNE, ALFORD & STRATHDON, 1:25,000 » **REFRESHMENTS:** LOCH KINORD HOTEL, DINNET » **NAVIGATION:** STRAIGHTFORWARD.

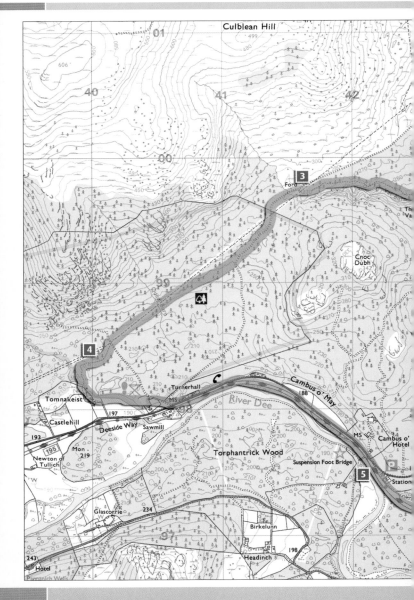

16 THE MUIR OF DINNET & THE VAT BURN

Directions – The Muir of Dinnet & the Vat Burn

⑤▶ From the car park **head past the Visitor Centre** and **bear left** passing the toilets. Soon **cross a footbridge** over the Vat Burn. Ignore the next footbridge on the right, **continuing ahead** up the path signed *Spur Path to The Vat*. At the end of the path, **continue ahead over rocks** and using stepping stones enter The Vat. At times of very high water this may not be possible, but normally the scramble into The Vat can be done with dry feet.

2 The only safe way out of The Vat is back via the narrow entrance – inevitably you will meet someone coming the other way and have to dance around on the stepping stones. Once safely back on the path **head back down to the bridge** and **turn left** to cross it. **Climb the steps** on the far side and **bear right** at the top to follow the path through the woods. At a T-junction **turn left** (there is a sign pointing right for the car park) and keep on the main path which begins climbing uphill.

3 Eventually a clearing with telegraph poles is crossed and a T-junction reached. **Turn left** signed for *Cambus O' May*. The old track climbs over a low pass and begins to descend. **Continue straight ahead** past a sign and gate to head into a forestry plantation. Here the trees have been thinned to allow a healthy understorey of blaeberry and heather to grow, providing the ideal habitat for the endangered capercaillie. At a junction, with a lochan visible to the left, **fork right** on to a smaller path, still waymarked in yellow. Soon **keep ahead to cross a footbridge** over the Queel Burn and at a clearing **keep straight on** at a crosspaths.

4 Head through mixed woodland and **bear right at a fork** soon climbing up on to a ridge, or esker, formed by a retreating glacier. At the end of this the path reaches the Cambus O' May car park. **Keep ahead**, following the track as it bends left and then **bear right** to follow the car park access track to reach the A93 at a bus stop. **Cross the A93** and join the Deeside Way on the far side and turn left. This flat and straight path follows the line of the old Royal Deeside Railway that once ran from Aberdeen to Ballater via Aboyne. The path soon runs alongside the River Dee; past a cottage go **through a gate** and continue past the white Cambus O' May Suspension Bridge.

5 **Continue ahead** passing an old station building and following a long section through birch, aspen and pine woods. **Keep straight ahead** for more than 3km until the buildings of Dinnet are visible. **Fork left** on a path to reach the main road and cross to the car park opposite. **Bear left** to pick up a path heading away from the far left-hand corner of the car park, passing behind the chalets of the Loch Kinord Hotel.

6 Pass the remains of a bird hide overlooking a tiny lochan and **bear right to cross a footbridge**. **Keep right** to pass a viewing platform over a larger lochan and stay by the waterside to follow a path waymarked with red arrows. Follow a line of telegraph poles and **go through a double set of walkers' gates** and at the Muir of Dinnet National Nature Reserve turn right on to a grassy path. **Follow the blue duck waymarkers** to eventually reach the edge of Loch Kinord. Keep following these waymarkers, eventually climbing to a finely carved ninth-century Pictish stone.

7 **Head uphill** past the stone before bearing left on a grassy track (still following duck waymarkers). **Keep left** when the route forks and stay on the main path which meanders through woods. At a commemorative plaque **continue ahead**, still following the waymarkers, and soon passing a vehicle barrier. **Bear right** at a fork and **turn left** at a waymarker before **turning right** and crossing the road to return to the start.

THE VAT

GLEN QUOICH

17 Clais Fhearnaig Circuit

16.3km/10.1miles

A hidden cleft through the hills links two of the finest glens in the southern Cairngorms.

Linn of Quoich » Glen Quoich » Clais Fhearnaig » Glen Lui » Claybokie » Victoria Bridge »
Linn of Quoich

Start

End of public road, Linn of Quoich.
GR: NO 117910.

The Walk

The route begins near The Punch Bowl at the Linn of Quoich, a quieter but no less beautiful spot than the nearby Linn of Dee. This stone bowl was carved over the centuries by the force of the Quoich Water, its fame resting on the Earl of Mar who is said to have filled it to the brim in order to toast the Jacobite cause in 1715. The Punch Bowl actually has a hole in the bottom but, whatever the truth, the view from the footbridge deserves a place in local legend.

A track leads up into Glen Quoich, perhaps the most beautiful of the glens branching off Deeside. Due to the enlightened management of the National Trust for Scotland, the Caledonian pinewoods here are regenerating once more, and there are many young trees springing up alongside the old, a perfect foreground to views of the mountains. Higher up the glen the route cuts off on an old path that aims for an almost-hidden pass, the Clais Fhearnaig. A gentle climb leads past a beautiful lochan enclosed between steep slopes.

A short climb beyond this and the high point of the walk is reached. The views here towards the heart of the Cairngorms massif are tremendous, as is the outlook down Glen Lui. The descent is straightforward and a track then leads down the glen, eventually back amongst pines. A beautiful section keeps high through the woods before reaching the entrance driveway to Mar Lodge, headquarters for the Trust's vast estate of the same name. The route now joins the River Dee, with views towards this impressive Scottish Baronial pile. Eventually a mixture of tracks, paths and a minor road leads back to the start at the Linn of Quoich.

CLAIS FHEARNAIG CIRCUIT

DISTANCE: 16.3KM/10.1MILES » **TOTAL ASCENT:** 321M/1,053FT » **START GR:** NO 117910 » **TIME:** ALLOW 4.5 HOURS
SATNAV: AB35 5YJ » **MAP:** OS EXPLORER 58, BRAEMAR, TOMINTOUL & GLEN AVON, 1:25,000 » **REFRESHMENTS:** NONE ON
ROUTE, NEAREST FIFE ARMS OR TASTE CAFE, BRAEMAR » **NAVIGATION:** STRAIGHTFORWARD.

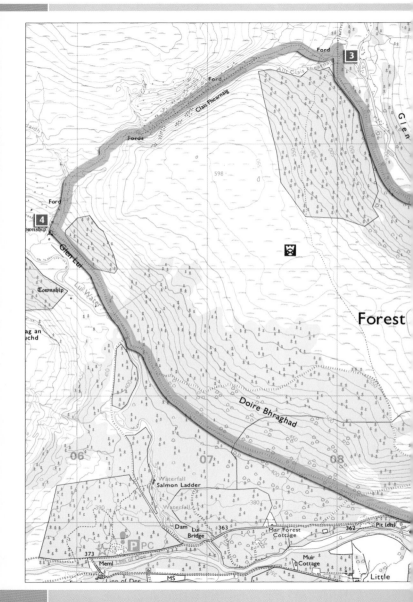

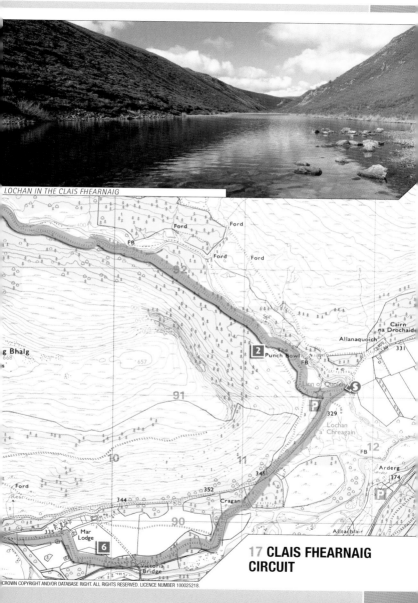

LOCHAN IN THE CLAIS FHEARNAIG

17 CLAIS FHEARNAIG CIRCUIT

Directions – Clais Fhearnaig Circuit

⟳ From the parking area walk towards the bridge but before it is reached turn **sharp left** on to the footpath heading uphill. **Turn right** at the crossroads to head downhill to the beautiful Linn of Quoich. Follow the track down through the trees to reach the bridge from where there is a good view of The Punch Bowl just upstream. This is a lovely spot to linger but this route doesn't cross the river, instead **turn back** and retrace the track uphill and **keep straight ahead** on to a path where the track bends sharp left.

2 Soon the main track heading up Glen Quoich is joined; **turn right** to follow it. The route passes amongst scattered pines. Ignore a footbridge over the Quoich Water seen down on the right; the track itself eventually runs closer to the river. **Continue ahead** as the views of the mountains come into view with the massive Beinn A' Bhuird, sprinkled with granite tors, prominent.

3 Ignore a track off to the left. Immediately after crossing the Allt Clais Fhearnaig **turn left** on to a small path. The path soon improves and climbs over moorland towards the narrow defile that is the Clais Fhearnaig pass. From the Gaelic meaning 'hollow place of the alders', there are no trees now; but a tranquil lochan, dammed to provide trout fishing, makes a good spot for a break. After the lochan, **continue to climb** for a short distance to the high point of the pass where there are views into Glen Lui. Follow the path downhill until it eventually reaches the track at the bottom of the glen.

4 **Turn left** to head away from the main mountains of the Cairngorms. At Black Bridge do not cross the river, instead **head straight on** and follow the track by the river. Soon it climbs uphill into Doire Bhraghad woods. **Keep straight ahead** when tracks lead off left and right, eventually descending to meet the tarmac road at Claybokie.

5 **Turn left here**, and then very soon **branch right** to take the lane for Mar Lodge. Near the river, **bear right** to go through the walkers' gate and **aim left** to follow the path downstream. Follow the Dee until a wide bend in the river, then **turn left** at a way marker following an indistinct path between a fence and pine trees. Mar Lodge soon comes into view on the left. At a grassy track **branch right** to return to the riverbank with Victoria Bridge visible up ahead.

6 Before the bridge **turn left** on to a waymarked path and cross a footbridge and go through a gate. **Turn right** on to a road and at the next junction go **straight ahead** on to a track through trees. Ignore a track on the left and eventually go through a farm gate to pass in front of the house at Cragan. At the road **turn right** to return to the start at the Linn of Quoich.

PINES OF GLEN QUOICH

LOCHNAGAR

18 **Lochnagar & Loch Muick**

19km/11.8miles

One of the finest and best-known mountains in the region.

Spittal of Glenmuick » Bealeach between Conachcraig and Meikle Pap » Lochnagar Corrie Headwall » Lochnagar Summit » Falls of the Glasallt » Loch Muick » Spittal of Glenmuick

Start

Car park, Glen Muick road end (parking charge). GR: NO 309851.

The Walk

This circuit is a Scottish hill classic, ascending via a spectacular corrie to reach a peaked summit with one of the finest views in the land.

The route begins from the car park at the end of the road up Glen Muick, crossing the glen below Loch Muick, a favourite royal playground since Queen Victoria's time. Lochnagar remains hidden from view as a track climbs up past some Balmoral Estate buildings and up through a pinewood and then over moorland.

Reaching the bealach between Lochnagar and the Meikle Pap is a magical moment, as here the character of the scenery changes completely and the sheer grandeur of Lochnagar is revealed. The northern corrie is a huge glacial scoop cradling the loch that gives the mountain its name, backed by great granite cliffs. 'Dark Lochanagar' was celebrated in verse by Lord Byron, who wrote

'England! thy beauties are tame and domestic, / To one who has rov'd on the mountains afar; / Oh! for the crags that are wild and majestic, / The steep, frowning glories of dark Loch na Garr!'

The ascent steepens considerably up a bouldery slope on a section known as the Ladder, prone to avalanches in winter. Above this is the summit plateau – the route continues around the rim of the cliffs before the final pull to the trig point at Cac Carn Beag. The reward is stupendous views in all directions.

Queen Victoria herself made the ascent here, but did not seem so impressed as Byron. She wrote of her summit experience as 'cold, and wet, and cheerless' – a familiar experience for any regular hillwalker! The return route descends steeply alongside the tumbling Glas Allt waterfalls to emerge next to the Royal Lodge Glas-allt-Shiel on Loch Muick.

LOCHNAGAR & LOCH MUICK

DISTANCE: 19KM/11.8MILES » **TOTAL ASCENT:** 930M/3,051FT » **START GR:** NO 309851 » **TIME:** ALLOW 7 HOURS **SATNAV:** AB35 5SU » **MAP:** OS EXPLORER 53, LOCHNAGAR, GLEN MUICK & GLEN CLOVA, 1:25,000 » **REFRESHMENTS:** NONE ON ROUTE, NEAREST BALLATER » **NAVIGATION:** MOSTLY GOOD HILL PATHS IN CLEAR CONDITIONS BUT MAP-READING SKILLS ESSENTIAL; ASCENT ROUTE NEEDS EXTREME CARE IN WINTER CONDITIONS.

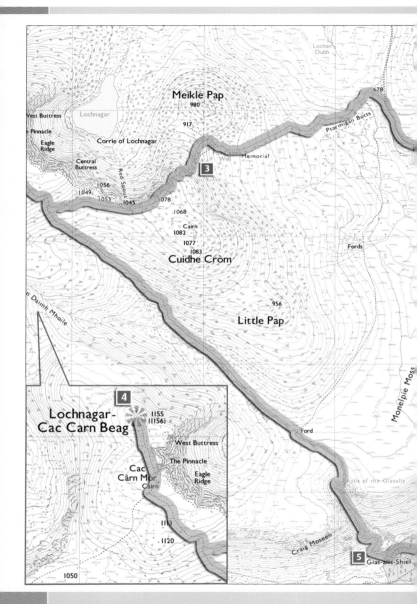

18 LOCHNAGAR & LOCH MUICK

Directions – Lochnagar & Loch Muick

➎ From the car park **follow the track** past the visitor centre and toilets at the Spittal of Glenmuick. After the trees **turn right** and cross the River Muick. On the far side of the glen **go straight across** the track and take the path to the right of the Balmoral Estate buildings which soon climbs up through woods.

2 **Cross the Allt na Guibhsaich** at the ford and continue climbing the track ahead as it eventually bends to the right after passing a small gorge. Near the col between Conachcraig on the right and Meikle Pap on the left, **fork left** on to a well-made path. Just before the bealach between Cuidhe Cròm and Meikle Pap, **branch left** on to the path leading to Lochnagar.

> **OR** If time allows it is really worth making a detour to climb Meikle Pap which has an unrivalled view of the Lochnagar crags. **Continue ahead** to the bealach and **bear right** to reach the summit.

3 **Climb steeply up** the section known as the Ladder, the path helps find a way through the boulders and eventually the gradient eases. **Bear right** towards the plateau keeping well back from the cliff edge and follow the headwall of the corrie. **Climb a short section** and soon the cairn marking the minor summit of Cac Càrn Mòr is reached. **Continue ahead** to the trig point with viewpoint indicator at the true summit of Lochnagar, Cac Carn Beag.

4 From the summit **retrace the route back to Cac Càrn Mòr** and from here **head south-east** down the slope to reach the upper reaches of the Glas Allt Glen. Keep on the path as it **heads down the left-hand side of the stream** at first and then crossing to the right-hand side. The path steepens as it stays close to the stream which now cascades down the hillside in a series of waterfalls.

5 Eventually the trees sheltering the Royal Lodge of Glas-allt-Shiel is reached. The path **bears left** to cross back over the Glas Allt and eventually reaches the lochside track to the left of the lodge. **Turn left** to head alongside Loch Muick. At a Boat House **turn right** to follow a path that passes in front of it. **Cross a footbridge** and stay on the path as it leaves the lochside and eventually reaches a track. **Turn left** on to the track which leads back to the Spittal of Glenmuick and the start.

THE TRACK DOWN FROM THE SUMMIT OF MORRONE

19 **Morrone from Braemar** 12km/7.5miles

Morrone is very much Braemar's hill; the climb up through nature-rich birchwoods rewards with superb views into the Cairngorms.

Braemar » Braemar Duck Pond » Viewpoint » Morrone Summit » West Ridge » Old Military Road » Braemar

Start

Balnellan Road car park, Braemar.
GR: NO 151913.

The Walk

The picturesque village of Braemar lies 339 metres above sea level, bringing the superb views from the summit of Morrone at 859 metres within range of a modest hillwalk without too much effort. Passing a number of old cottages and Victorian villas, the route passes near the grounds used to host the annual Braemar Gathering, a traditional Highland Games usually attended by members of the Royal Family. The Braemar Gathering features a hill race up and down Morrone.

Beyond the Braemar Duck Pond a track leads into Morrone Birkwood, one of the UK's finest remaining tracts of 'downy' birchwood, with extensive areas of juniper. This is a special area of conservation for its rich flora, which in springtime includes the rare twinflower and globeflower.

Above the trees a path climbs steeply to a viewpoint over Braemar and then continues up on to open moorland, ascending steadily until the mast on the summit is seen in the distance.

The path crosses stony ground as the gradient eases for the long final pull to the top. Morrone is one of Scotland's 222 Corbetts – hills between 2,500 and 3,000 feet with 500 feet of descent on all sides. From the summit there are fabulous views in all directions, but that towards the main mass of the Cairngorms is a classic.

The descent route follows a stony track down the broad ridge. Eventually it swings eastwards to descend to the minor road which runs alongside the Clunie Water. This quiet lane is followed for the walk back to the village, providing lovely views of the river.

MORRONE FROM BRAEMAR

DISTANCE: 12KM/7.5MILES » **TOTAL ACCENT:** 650M/2,132FT » **START GR:** NO 151913 » **TIME:** ALLOW 5 HOURS » **SATNAV:** AB35 5YE » **MAP:** OS EXPLORER 52, GLEN SHEE & BRAEMAR, 1:25,000 » **REFRESHMENTS:** FIFE ARMS OR TASTE CAFE, BRAEMAR » **NAVIGATION:** STRAIGHTFORWARD.

Directions – Morrone from Braemar

⑤ Begin at the car park in the centre of Braemar with public toilets; **take the main road** through the village, crossing the bridge over the Clunie Water and passing the Fife Arms. Once past the village hall **bear left** at the roundabout, taking the second exit to **go straight ahead** up Chapel Brae. Continue to Braemar Duck Pond, and past the last house on to a track signed *Morrone*.

2 **Branch left** at a fork and go through a gate as the track continues uphill. After passing a house on the left, **bear right and then left** on the track to climb more steeply. **Fork left** through the trees and scrub to arrive at a viewpoint indicator and bench. Cross the track, to take a path signed *Morrone*.

3 **Go through a gate** as the path climbs through heather moorland with good views back over Braemar. Eventually as height is gained the path becomes stonier underfoot and the summit of Morrone looms into view a fair distance ahead. **Bear left** on the path before the final pull to the trig point and buildings at the top. At 859m Morrone is a great vantage point over Braemar and much of upper Deeside as well as to the surrounding higher mountains.

4 For the descent, **take the track heading south–west**, descending downhill gently to a slight bealach. The track then turns south-east to climb slightly over the 824m high point. Further on, follow the track when it **bears left** downhill. It descends steadily, zigzagging a number of times before eventually reaching the glen floor.

5 **Turn left** on to the minor road which runs alongside a delightful stretch of the Clunie Water. **Continue ahead** over a cattle grid and pass Braemar Golf Club to reach the outlying houses of the village. The road reaches the centre of Braemar next to the bridge. **Turn right** to cross the river and **right again** back into the car park.

19 MORRONE FROM BRAEMAR

DERRY CAIRNGORM FROM THE LINN OF DEE

DISTANCE: 26.8KM/16.7MILES » **TOTAL ASCENT:** 829M/2,720FT » **START GR:** NO 062898 » **TIME:** ALLOW 9 HOURS » **SATNAV:** AB35 5YB » **MAP:** OS EXPLORER 57, CAIRN GORM & AVIEMORE, 1:25,000 » **REFRESHMENTS:** NONE ON ROUTE, NEAREST FIFE ARMS OR TASTE CAFE, BRAEMAR » **NAVIGATION:** EXTREMELY REMOTE AND EXPOSED TO POOR WEATHER, WITH SOME BOULDERY GROUND; GOOD NAVIGATION AND HILLWALKING SKILLS NEEDED.

GLEN DERRY

Derry Cairngorm from the Linn of Dee

26.8km/16.7miles

This remote and bouldery granite cone offers a grand mountain walk into the wild heart of the Cairngorms National Park.

Linn of Dee » Derry Lodge » Carn Crom » Derry Cairngorm » Loch Etchachan » Glen Derry » Derry Lodge » Linn of Dee

Start

Linn of Dee car park (parking charge). GR: NO 062898.

The Walk

This long but satisfying hillwalk gives a real flavour of all the defining characteristics of the Cairngorms. The walking is rough, with some boulderfields to cross and burns to ford; it's a challenging day out in truly remote country. A mountain bike can be taken as far as Derry Lodge to shorten the day.

The route starts at the spectacular Linn of Dee, where the river is forced through a narrow gorge, before heading up wide Glen Lui towards the mountains. This first section of track is popular as the starting point for a number of Munros, mountain biking and multiday camping or bothying expeditions, as well as being part of the Lairig Ghru foot pass leading through to Speyside. However, the area never feels busy as people are quickly lost amongst the vast scale of the Cairngorms.

From the pines surrounding Derry Lodge the route crosses a footbridge over the Derry Burn before climbing through the pines. Once beyond the tree line the path climbs almost to the summit of Carn Crom – worth a detour to take in the views of Cairn Toul and Braeriach. After a slight dip there is a long ascent to Derry Cairngorm, the uppermost slopes rising as a great stony dome.

From the summit the longer descent route crosses boulder fields at first, eventually descending more steeply to reach Loch Etchachan – an extremely remote and surprisingly large loch at more than 900 metres above sea level. The route follows the outflow of the loch, passing the Hutchison Memorial Hut, a remote bothy, or open shelter, used by walkers (if you use it, be sure to leave it clean and tidy). The long hike down Glen Derry is a real delight, though the Glas Allt Mòr has no bridge and can be impassable in spate. Further down the glen the walk leads through some of Scotland's most beautiful pinewoods before the route returns to Derry Lodge and retraces the final leg back to the Linn of Dee.

Directions – Derry Cairngorm from the Linn of Dee

↪ From the Linn of Dee car park take the footpath at the back of the parking area through the trees, signed *Glen Lui*. **Descend steps** and cross a boardwalk; go through a gate and up a slope. **Turn left** along a track and cross Black Bridge over the Lui Water. **Turn left** on to the main track up the glen. **Continue ahead** along this until the pinewoods around Derry Lodge are reached.

2 Built as a shooting lodge, and reputed to have been used by Queen Victoria, Derry Lodge now belongs to the National Trust for Scotland but is currently disused. If cycling leave your bike here. **Keep straight on,** passing a hut and **cross the footbridge** over the Derry Burn. Ignore paths to the left and right and **keep straight ahead** and soon the path heads up through the trees to climb Creag Bad an t-Seabhaig. Keep heading uphill as the route becomes less steep. At 840m you can detour half-left (north-west) to the summit of Carn Crom for the view; otherwise continue on the path. The path descends slightly to a shallow bealach and then climbs over increasingly rocky ground. **Keep to the right** (east) of the first top, marked with a cairn, and continue over the small, rounded boulders to reach the summit cairn of Derry Cairngorm at 1,155m.

ON CARN CROM

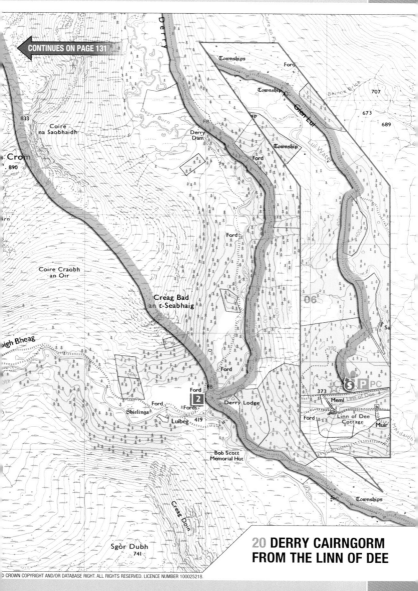

Map labels:

← CONTINUES ON PAGE 131

Townships
Ford
Townships
Glen Lui
833
Coire na Saobhaidh
Lui Water
707
673
689
Crom
890
Derry Dam
Derry Burn
Ford
Township
Ford
Ford
Coire Craobh an Oir
06
Creag Bad an t-Seabhaig
Ford
igh Bheag
Ford
Ford
373
P PC
6
Mem Linn of Dee
2
Ford
Fords
Derry Lodge
Ford
Linn of Dee Cottage
Shielings
Luibeg
419
Muir
Bob Scott Memorial Hut
Townships
Creag Dhu
Sgòr Dubh
741

20 DERRY CAIRNGORM FROM THE LINN OF DEE

3 **Aim half-left** to bear north-west from the summit and then north-north-west to descend the broad, pathless and boulder-covered ridge. **Keep straight ahead** at the bealach to pass to the west side of Creagan a' Choire Etchachan. Just beyond here **turn right** on to the path between Ben Macdui and Loch Etchachan.

4 **Fork right** just before Little Loch Etchachan to follow a path alongside the burn and descend into Coire Etchachan. Continue past the Hutchison Memorial Hut, a remote shelter maintained by volunteers from the Mountain Bothy Association. Continue downhill, and 1km beyond the hut **cross a bridge** over the Coire Etchachan Burn.

5 Further on the Lairig an Laoigh route joins from the left; **continue down the glen;** soon the Glas Allt Mòr is reached, **which must be crossed**. There is no bridge and if water levels are very high it can be completely impassable. In drier conditions it can be crossed on stones or with a shallow wade. **Continue ahead,** staying on the east side of the river to eventually reach Derry Lodge. **Bear left** to pass the lodge and return along the Glen Lui track back to the Linn of Dee.

LOOKING BACK DOWN OVER THE DERRY

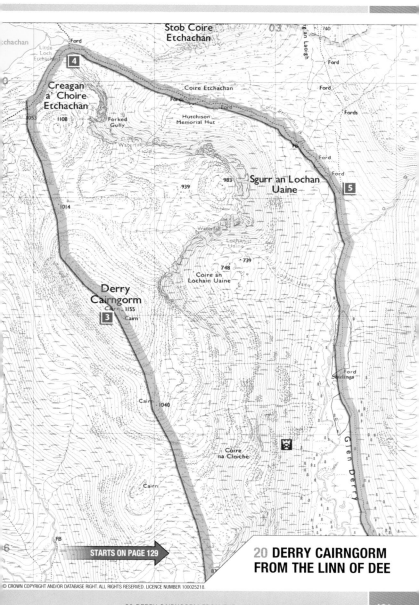

STARTS ON PAGE 129

20 DERRY CAIRNGORM FROM THE LINN OF DEE

Appendix

The following is a list of Visitor Information Centres, shops, cafes, pubs, websites and other contacts that might come in handy.

Visitor Information Centres

www.visitcairngorms.com

Aviemore	T: 01479 810 930
Ballater	T: 01339 755 306
Crathie	T: 01339 742 414
Grantown-on-Spey	T: 01479 872 478
Tomintoul	T: 01807 580 285

Food & Drink
Cafes

Sugar Bowl Cafe .... T: 01540 661 641
Kingussie
Old Post Office Cafe .... T: 01540 651 779
Kincraig
The Druie .... T: 01479 812 345
Rothiemurchus Centre
Mountain Cafe .... T: 01479 812 473
Aviemore
Cobbs Cafe .... T: 0131 370 5965
Glenmore Visitor Centre
The High Street Merchants .... T: 01479 872 246
Grantown-on-Spey
Nethy House, Nethy Bridge .. T: 07963 217 793
Taste Cafe, Braemar .... T: 01339 741 425

Pubs

The Glen Hotel, Newtonmore .. T: 01540 673 203
The Glenavon, Tomintoul ...... T: 01807 580 218
Loch Kinord Hotel, Dinnet ..... T: 01339 885 229
Fife Arms, Braemar .... T: 01339 720 200

Accommodation
Bed & Breakfast, Hotels, Cottages and Campsites

www.visitcairngorms.com/accommodation

Hostels & Bunkhouses

Hostelling Scotland .... T: 0345 293 7373
www.hostellingscotland.org.uk
Scottish Independent Hostels
www.hostel-scotland.co.uk

Bothies

Mountain Bothies Association
www.mountainbothies.org.uk

Weather

www.mwis.org.uk
www.metoffice.gov.uk
www.smidgeup.com/midge-forecast

Other Contacts

www.outdooraccess-scotland.scot
www.forestryandland.gov.scot
www.nature.scot/enjoying-outdoors

Outdoor Shops

Braemar Mountain Sports ..... T: 01339 741 242
Ballater and Braemar
www.braemarmountainsports.com
Nevisport .... T: 01479 810 239
Aviemore, www.nevisport.com
Ellis Brigham .... T: 01479 810 175
Aviemore, www.ellis-brigham.com
Cairngorm Mountain Sports .... T: 01339 741 242
Aviemore, www.braemarmountainsports.com

Other Publications

Scottish Island Bagging
Helen and Paul Webster, Vertebrate Publishing
www.v-publishing.co.uk

Scotland Mountain Biking – The Wild Trails
Phil McKane, Vertebrate Publishing
www.v-publishing.co.uk

Scotland Mountain Biking – Wild Trails Vol.2
Phil McKane, Vertebrate Publishing
www.v-publishing.co.uk

About the Authors

Helen and Paul Webster share a passion for walking and wild places. In 2003–2004 they undertook a life-changing 4,000-mile continuous backpacking trip across Europe. Following their return, they quit their careers to begin a new life evangelising for Scotland's spectacular outdoors – especially the Highlands and Islands. Together they set up Walkhighlands, a free online guide and forum which has become the busiest walkers' website in the UK. They have also written seventeen guidebooks to various areas of Scotland, including *Scottish Island Bagging,* and in 2018 Paul won the Scottish Landscape Photographer of the Year competition. They live in the Cairngorms National Park.
www.walkhighlands.co.uk

Vertebrate Publishing

At Vertebrate Publishing we publish books to inspire adventure.

It's our rule that the only books we publish are those that we'd want to read or use ourselves. We endeavour to bring you beautiful books that stand the test of time and that you'll be proud to have on your bookshelf for years to come.

The Peak District was the inspiration behind our first books. Our offices are situated on its doorstep, minutes away from world-class climbing, biking and hillwalking. We're driven by our own passion for the outdoors, for exploration, and for the natural world; it's this passion that we want to share with our readers.

We aim to inspire everyone to get out there. We want to connect readers – young and old – with the outdoors and the positive impact it can have on well-being. We think it's particularly important that young people get outside and explore the natural world, something we support through our publishing programme.

As well as publishing award-winning new books, we're working to make available many out-of-print classics in both print and digital formats. These are stories that we believe are unique and significant; we want to make sure that they continue to be shared and enjoyed.
www.v-publishing.co.uk

VP DAY WALKS GUIDEBOOKS

Written by local authors, each pocket-sized guidebook features:

Map data

- 20 great day-length walks
- Ordnance Survey 1:25,000-scale maps
- easy-to-follow directions
- distance & navigation information
- refreshment stops & local area information
- detailed appendix

1 DAY WALKS IN THE CAIRNGORMS

2 DAY WALKS IN SNOWDONIA

3 DAY WALKS IN THE BRECON BEACONS

4 DAY WALKS ON THE PEMBROKESHIRE COAST

5 DAY WALKS IN THE LAKE DISTRICT

6 DAY WALKS IN THE YORKSHIRE DALES

7 DAYS WALKS IN THE NORTH YORK MOORS

8 DAY WALKS IN THE PEAK DISTRICT

9 DAY WALKS IN THE PEAK DISTRICT

10 DAY WALKS IN THE COTSWOLDS

11 DAY WALKS IN DEVON

12 DAY WALKS IN CORNWALL

13 DAY WALKS ON THE HIGH WEALD

14 DAY WALKS ON THE SOUTH DOWNS

Available from book shops or direct from:
www.v-publishing.co.uk